RADIO AND TELEVISION PIONEERS:

a patent bibliography

by

DAVID W. KRAEUTER

The Scarecrow Press, Inc.
Metuchen, N.J., & London
1992

British Library Cataloguing-in-Publication data available

Library of Congress Cataloging-in-Publication Data

Kraeuter, David W.
      Radio and television pioneers : a patent bibliography / by
David W. Kraeuter.
            p.   cm.
      Includes indexes.
      ISBN 0-8108-2556-2 (acid-free paper)
      1. Radio—United States—Apparatus and supplies—
Patents—Bibliography. 2. Television—United States—
Equipment and supplies—Patents—Bibliography.
3. Inventors—United States—Bibliography. I. Title.
Z7224.U6K7   1992
[TK6553]
016.621384'027273—dc20   92-8879

Dedicated to the inventors.

PREFACE

This book can be of use to anyone studying the technical history of radio and television, particularly as it developed in the United States. Over 3000 U.S. patents are cited, listed in chronological order under the name of the inventor. This arrangement provides a sense of the historical development of each inventor's work.

The choice of inventors to include was entirely my own, and ranges from the creative genius of Edwin Armstrong to the relative obscurity of Joseph Murgas. A few inventors listed here worked largely outside the field of electronics. They were included because of their strong connections with the early development of radio—H. P. Davis as a founder of KDKA and H. P. Maxim as a founder of the American Radio Relay League are examples.

Edison's and Tesla's patents have already been published in complete editions. See *Patents Granted to Thomas A. Edison, 1869-1918* (Washington, DC: Microfilm Publications, National Archives, 1981) and J. T. Ratzlaff, ed., *Dr. Nikola Tesla, Complete Patents* (Millbrae, CA: Tesla Book Co., 1983).

Although some of these inventors also patented their devices in other countries, only U.S. patents are listed here.

Most of this information was collated from various indexes published by the U.S. Patent Office. For a list of these, see Eugene P. Sheehy's *Guide to Reference Books*, 10th edition (Chicago: American Library Association, 1986), p. 1155.

Patent indexes in various volumes of the Congressional serial set were also consulted for material prior to 1872. See

Tables of and Annotated Index to the Congressional Series of United States Public Documents (Washington: U.S. GPO, 1902), pp. 556-560.

I thank the Antique Wireless Association and Ludwell Sibley for publishing sections of the manuscript in the *AWA Review*. Thanks also to Beverley Martin, who helped with proofreading, and Alan Douglas, who supplied some birth and death dates. Lastly I thank the staff of the Science and Technology Division of the Carnegie Library of Pittsburgh, where most of this information was gathered.

David W. Kraeuter
February, 1992
Washington, PA

USER'S GUIDE

For each inventor a chronological list of U.S. patents is provided. Citations take this form: *Title. Number. Date.* When the U.S. Patent Office's *Official Gazette* reference is known it follows the date and is given as *volume:page*, thus:

Space telegraphy. 879,532. February 18, 1908. 132:1458.

A title index is provided for each inventor with ten or more patents. It follows the chronological list.

The cumulated personal name index beginning on page 314 locates patents that were granted in the names of more than one person.

CONTENTS

(Number following name is total number of
patents listed for that inventor.)

ERNST ALEXANDERSON (1878-1975)

Synchronous motor. 785,532. March 21, 1905. 115:724.

Two-speed winding for three-phase motors. 785,533. March 21, 1905. 115:725.

Winding for three-phase motors. 785,995. March 28, 1905. 115:942.

Alternating-current generator. 789,404. May 9, 1905. 116:444.

Alternating-current generator. 789,476. May 9, 1905. 116:484.

Voltage-regulator. 805,253. November 21, 1905. 119:849.

Protective means for alternating-current systems. 819,627. May 1, 1906. 122:260.

Ground-detector and cut-out. 825,286. July 10, 1906. 123:327.

Means for controlling self-exciting generators. 829,133. August 21, 1906. 123:2462.

Voltage-regulator. 829,826. August 28, 1906. 123:2869.

Alternating-current generator. 839,358. December 25, 1906. 125:2503.

Motor-winding. 841,609. January 15, 1907. 126:1014.

Alternating-current motor. 841,610. January 15, 1907. 126:1016.

Dynamo-electric machine. 849,713. April 9, 1907. 127:2170.

Alternating-current motor. 859,358. July 9, 1907. 129:579.

Frequency-changer. 859,359. July 9, 1907. 129:580.

Alternating-current motor. 861,012. July 23, 1907. 129:1472.

Dynamo-electric machine. 861,072. July 23, 1907. 129:1496.

Induction-motor. 872,550. December 3, 1907. 131:1244.

Alternating-current motor. 873,702. December 17, 1907. 131:1693.

Starting motor-converter. 876,923. January 21, 1908. 132:481.

Compensated motor. 876,924. January 21, 1908. 132:481.

Self-excited alternator. 881,647. March 10, 1908. 133:415.

Induction-motor control. 882,606. March 24, 1908. 133:787.

Motor control. 885,128. April 21, 1908. 133:1727.

Self-exciting generator. 895,933. August 11, 1908. 135:1297. [With E. H. Widegren.]

Synchronous motor. 897,507. September 1, 1908. 136:87.

Alternating-current motor. 897,508. September 1, 1908. 136:87.

Induction-motor control. 901,513. October 20, 1908. 136:1608.

Telephone-relay. 902,195. October 27, 1908. 136:1858.

Alternating-current high-frequency generator. 905,621. December 1, 1908. 137:1147.

Electric motor. 919,514. April 27, 1909. 141:946.

Single-phase motor. 920,710. May 4, 1909. 142:203.

Induction-generator. 920,809. May 4, 1909. 142:235.

Alternating-current motor. 920,896. May 4, 1909. 142:262.

System of electric distribution. 921,786. May 18, 1909. 142:620.

Electric motor. 923,311. June 1, 1909. 143:66.

Single-phase-motor control. 923,312. June 1, 1909. 143:67.

Alternating-current motor. 923,753. June 1, 1909. 143:219.

Alternating-current motor. 923,754. June 1, 1909. 143:219.

Single-phase-motor control. 927,397. July 6, 1909. 144:230.

Alternating-current motor. 927,398. July 6, 1909. 144:231.

Alternating-current-motor control. 927,399. July 6, 1909. 144:231.

Single-phase motor. 935,881. October 5, 1909. 147:87.

Motor control. 936,071. October 5, 1909. 147:150.

Motor-control system. 940,112. November 16, 1909. 148:630.

Alternating-current-motor control. 946,751. January 18, 1910. 150:648.

Dynamo-electric machine. 949,345. February 15, 1910. 151:577.

Single-phase-motor control. 949,346. February 15, 1910. 151:577.

Electric locomotive. 949,347. February 15, 1910. 151:578.

Commutator-motor. 949,992. February 22, 1910. 151:831.

Single-phase commutator-motor. 951,357. March 8, 1910. 152:319.

Single-phase commutator-motor. 953,366. March 29, 1910. 152:1080.

Overload protective device. 954,845. April 12, 1910. 153:429.

Motor control. 957,454. May 10, 1910. 154:356.

Braking alternating-current motors. 967,295. August 16, 1910. 157:541.

Electric braking. 967,296. August 16, 1910. 157:542.

Electric braking. 974,224. November 1, 1910. 160:45.

Motor control. 996,390. June 27, 1911. 167:889.

Reinforcer for telephone-circuits. 996,391. June 27, 1911. 167:890.

Telephone relay and system. 996,445. June 27, 1911. 167:908.

Manufacturing rotating bodies for high-speed machinery. 998,734. July 25, 1911. 168:846.

High-frequency alternator. 1,008,577. November 14, 1911. 172:367.

Alternating-current motor. 1,019,402. March 5, 1912. 176:136.

Single-phase motor. 1,021,289. March 26, 1912. 176:885.

Method of and apparatus for relaying high-frequency currents. 1,042,069. October 22, 1912. 183:910.

Alternating-current motor. 1,060,731. May 6, 1913. 190:58.

Alternating-current motor. 1,068,404. July 29, 1913. 192:997.

Means for compensating polyphase alternating-current commutation-motors. 1,080,403. December 2, 1913. 197:172.

Air-inlet valve for carbureters [sic]. 1,083,789. January 6, 1914. 198:174.

Electric braking with alternating-current motors. 1,089,384. March 3, 1914. 200:240.

Dynamo-electric machine. 1,091,613. March 31, 1914. 200:1170.

Dynamo-electric machine. 1,091,614. March 31, 1914. 200:1171.

Dynamo-electric machine. 1,092,420. April 7, 1914. 201:102.

Phase-balancer. 1,093,594. April 21, 1914. 201:575.

Alternating-current-motor control. 1,098,656. June 2, 1914. 203:102.

Method of and apparatus for indicating the speed of electric motors. 1,100,280. June 16, 1914. 203:737.

Telephone system. 1,102,628. July 7, 1914. 204:143.

High-frequency alternator. 1,110,028. September 8, 1914. 206:455.

High-frequency alternator. 1,110,029. September 8, 1914. 206:456.

Bearing. 1,110,030. September 8, 1914. 206:456.

Induction-motor. 1,119,741. December 1, 1914. 209:288.

Neutralizing inductive disturbances. 1,120,992. December 15, 1914. 209:811.

High-frequency alternator. 1,126,334. January 26, 1915. 210:1222.

System of electrical distribution. 1,150,652. August 17, 1915. 217:936.

Split-phase system. 1,170,211. February 1, 1916. 223:161.

Selective tuning system. 1,173,079. February 22, 1916. 223:1312.

Boiler and heating arrangement therefor. 1,174,375. March 7, 1916. 224:123.

Frequency transformation. 1,174,793. March 7, 1916. 224:280.

Phase-balancer. Reissue 14,133. May 16, 1916. 226:1046.

Induction-motor. 1,185,461. May 30, 1916. 226:1709.

Alternating-current motor. 1,194,265. August 8, 1916. 229:546.

Alternating-current-commutator motor. 1,194,923. August 15, 1916. 229:821.

Controlling alternating currents. 1,206,643. November 28, 1916. 232:1175.

High-speed rotating body. 1,208,441. December 12, 1916. 233:624.

System of ship propulsion. 1,215,094. February 6, 1917. 235:214.

System of ship propulsion. 1,215,095. February 6, 1917. 235:215.

Power-transmitting mechanism. 1,223,924. April 24, 1917. 237:1125.

High-frequency alternator. 1,229,856. June 12, 1917. 239:548.

Automatic control of phase-converters. 1,233,952. July 17, 1917. 240:862.

Regulator for phase-balancers. 1,233,953. July 17, 1917. 240:863.

System of electrical distribution. 1,242,632. October 9, 1917. 243:410.

Apparatus for producing an electromotive force of special wave form. 1,250,752. December 18, 1917. 245:748.

Internal-combustion hydraulic pump. 1,259,338. March 12, 1918. 248:440.

Rotor for dynamo-electric machines. 1,261,673. April 2, 1918. 249:193.

Multispeed alternating-current motor. 1,263,992. April 23, 1918. 249:920.

Condenser. 1,266,377. May 14, 1918. 250:444.

Electrical system of power transmission. 1,268,662. June 4, 1918. 251:168.

Automatic control of phase-converters. Reissue 14,510. August 27, 1918. 253:921.

Motor-control system. 1,280,624. October 8, 1918. 255:167.

Motor excitation. 1,289,592. December 31, 1918. 257:956.

System of electric ship propulsion. 1,289,593. December 31, 1918. 257:956.

Series-multiple control. 1,300,542. April 15, 1919. 261:485.

System of phase modification. 1,300,543. April 15, 1919. 261:485.

System of phase modification. 1,300,544. April 15, 1919. 261:485.

Starting phase-converters. 1,300,545. April 15, 1919. 261:486.

Speed control of induction-motors. 1,301,632. April 22, 1919. 261:742. [With D. C. Prince.]

Electrical system of power transmission. 1,304,239. May 20, 1919. 262:393.

Electric system of ship propulsion. 1,304,240. May 20, 1919. 262:393. [With S. P. Nixdorff.]

Wireless-telephone system. 1,313,041. August 12, 1919. 265:258.

Wireless signaling system. 1,313,042. August 12, 1919. 265:258.

Bearing. 1,315,069. September 2, 1919. 266:109.

System of frequency transformation. 1,316,995. September 23, 1919. 266:537.

Radiosignaling system. 1,320,959. November 4, 1919. 268:113.

Means for controlling alternating currents. 1,328,473. January 20, 1920. 270:397.

Method of and means for controlling high-frequency alternating currents. 1,328,610. January 20, 1920. 270:423.

Means for controlling alternating currents. 1,328,797. January 20, 1920. 270:457.

Means for controlling alternating currents. 1,334,126. March 16, 1920. 272:481.

Regulating system for alternating-current circuits. 1,337,875. April 20, 1920. 273:546.

Method of and means for controlling electrical energy. 1,340,101. May 11, 1920. 274:348.

Wireless signaling system. 1,350,911. August 24, 1920. 277:711.

Radioreceiving system. 1,350,912. August 24, 1920. 277:711.

Antenna. 1,360,167. November 23, 1920. 280:732.

Antenna. 1,360,168. November 23, 1920. 280:732.

Radiosignaling system. 1,360,169. November 23, 1920. 280:732.

Series-multiple control. 1,365,441. January 11, 1921. 282:313.

High-frequency alternator. 1,366,627. January 25, 1921. 282:629.

High-frequency alternator. 1,369,601. February 22, 1921. 283:674.

Radio-receiving system. 1,373,931. April 5, 1921. 285:108.

System of electrical distribution. 1,375,991. April 26, 1921. 285:638.

Radio-receiving system. 1,375,992. April 26, 1921. 285:638.

Means for frequency transformations. 1,382,877. June 28, 1921. 287:650.

Cooling dynamo-electric machines. 1,382,878. June 28, 1921. 287:650.

Apparatus for producing and distributing electric-current waves of radio frequency. 1,386,830. August 9, 1921. 289:244.

System of radio communication. 1,400,847. December 20, 1921.

Removing sleet from antennae. 1,404,726. January 31, 1922.

Amplifying system. 1,419,797. June 13, 1922.

Rotary transforming apparatus. 1,420,398. June 20, 1922.

High-frequency alternator. 1,426,943. August 22, 1922.

Radiosignaling system. 1,426,944. August 22, 1922.

Control system. 1,461,571. July 10, 1923.

Unidirectional radio receiving system. 1,465,108. August 14, 1923.

Wireless signaling system. 1,465,961. August 28, 1923.

Wireless signaling system. 1,465,962. August 28, 1923.

High-frequency signaling system. 1,466,263. August 28, 1923.

Radio receiving system. 1,477,413. December 11, 1923.

Electric ship propulsion. 1,481,853. January 29, 1924.

Electric ship propulsion. 1,481,882. January 29, 1924.

System of motor control. 1,490,720. April 15, 1924.

Radio receiving system. 1,491,372. April 22, 1924.

Double-squirrel-cage synchronous motor. 1,495,969. May 27, 1924.

High-frequency signaling system. 1,500,785. July 8, 1924.

Wireless signaling system. 1,501,830. July 15, 1924.

Wireless signaling system. 1,501,831. July 15, 1924.

Wireless signaling system. 1,508,151. September 9, 1924.

Radio transmitting system. 1,517,816. December 2, 1924.

Controlling alternating currents. 1,522,221. January 6, 1925.

Electron-discharge device. 1,535,082. April 21, 1925.

System of distribution. 1,537,055. May 12, 1925.

Radio receiving system. 1,546,878. July 21, 1925.

Signaling system. 1,549,737. August 18, 1925.

Surge preventer. 1,554,698. September 22, 1925.

Operating electric motors. 1,563,004. November 24, 1925.

Radio signaling system. 1,564,807. December 8, 1925.

Electric ship propulsion. 1,579,051. March 30, 1925.

Transmitting angular motion. 1,600,204. September 14, 1926.

Alternating-current-motor control. 1,603,102. October 12, 1926.

High-frequency signaling system. 1,610,073. December 7, 1926.

System of distribution. 1,620,506. March 8, 1927.

Controlling alternating currents. 1,634,970. July 5, 1927.

High-frequency signaling system. 1,648,711. November 8, 1927.

Voltage regulator. 1,652,923. December 13, 1927.

Regulating system. 1,655,035. January 3, 1928.

Control of electric power. 1,655,036. January 3, 1928.

Locomotive control. 1,655,037. January 3, 1928.

Power-factor control system. 1,655,038. January 3, 1928.

Speed-control system. 1,655,039. January 3, 1928.

Control of electric power. 1,655,040. January 3, 1928.

Regulating apparatus. 1,655,041. January 3, 1928.

Speed-control system. 1,655,042. January 3, 1928.

Electric motor. 1,667,647. April 24, 1928.

Control system. 1,669,153. May 8, 1928.

System of electric ship propulsion. 1,676,312. July 10, 1928.

Antenna. 1,677,698. July 17, 1928.

System of electrical distribution. 1,677,699. July 17, 1928.

System of electrical distribution. 1,677,700. July 17, 1928.

System of distribution. 1,680,758. August 14, 1928.

Circuit-control apparatus. 1,691,423. November 13, 1928.

Electric apparatus. 1,694,244. December 4, 1928.

Electrical transmission of pictures. 1,694,301. December 4, 1928.

Transmission of pictures. 1,694,302. December 4, 1928.

Oscillation generator. 1,698,290. January 8, 1929.

Electric ship propulsion. 1,701,350. February 5, 1929.

Power-amplifying means. 1,706,094. March 19, 1929.

Rectifying apparatus. 1,718,515. June 25, 1929.

Control of electric power. 1,719,866. July 9, 1929.

Signaling system. 1,722,998. August 6, 1929.

System of ship propulsion. 1,723,906. August 6, 1929.

Radio receiving system. 1,723,907. August 6, 1929.

Ignition system. 1,723,908. August 6, 1929.

Speed-control system. 1,736,689. November 19, 1929.

Speed-indicating system. 1,747,041. February 11, 1930.

Transmission of pictures. 1,752,876. April 1, 1930.

Radiotelegraphy. 1,768,433. June 24, 1930.

Method of and apparatus for multiplex signaling. 1,771,700. July 29, 1930.

Stabilization of tuned radio frequency amplifiers. 1,775,544. September 9, 1930.

Radio signaling system. 1,775,801. September 16, 1930.

Transmission of pictures. 1,783,031. November 25, 1930.

Control system. 1,787,299. December 30, 1930.

Electric discharge device. 1,787,300. December 30, 1930.

Method and apparatus for picture transmission by wire or radio. 1,787,851. January 6, 1931. [With R. H. Ranger.]

Radio signaling system. 1,790,646. February 3, 1931.

Transmission of pictures. 1,792,264. February 10, 1931.

Radio signaling system. 1,797,039. March 17, 1931.

System of distribution. 1,800,002. April 7, 1931.

Radio signaling system. 1,814,813. July 14, 1931.

Transmission of pictures. 1,830,586. November 3, 1931.

System of distribution. 1,835,131. December 8, 1931.

Signaling. 1,839,455. January 5, 1932.

Eliminating fading. 1,853,021. April 12, 1932.

Picture transmission. 1,857,130. May 10, 1932.

System for producing high frequency oscillations. 1,866,337. July 5, 1932.

Picture transmission apparatus. 1,866,338. July 5, 1932.

Alternating current commutator machine. 1,867,396. July 12, 1932.

Signaling by phase displacement. 1,882,698. October 18, 1932.

Television receiver. 1,889,587. November 29, 1932.

Electrical system. 1,896,534. February 7, 1933.

Amplifying electrical impulses. 1,906,441. May 2, 1933. [With R. D. Kell.]

Indicating system for aircraft. 1,907,471. May 9, 1933.

Indicating altitude from aircraft. 1,913,148. June 6, 1933.

System of electric power transmission. 1,917,081. July 4, 1933.

System of electric power transmission. 1,917,082. July 4, 1933. [With P. L. Alger and S. P. Nixdorff.]

Radiant energy guiding system for airplanes. 1,917,114. July 4, 1933. [With John H. Hammond.]

Regenerative electric regulator. 1,917,146. July 4, 1933. [With S. P. Nixdorff.]

Electrical transmission system. 1,921,718. August 8, 1933.

Television apparatus. 1,935,427. November 14, 1933.

Electric valve converting system. 1,937,377. November 28, 1933.

Sound-motion picture producer. 1,937,378. November 28, 1933.

Electric valve converting system. 1,939,428. December 12, 1933.

Electric valve converting system. 1,939,429. December 12, 1933.

Electric valve excitation circuits. 1,954,661. April 10, 1934. [With A. H. Mittag and E. L. Phillipi.]

Automatic steering system. 1,958,258. May 8, 1934.

Method and means for determining altitude from aircraft. 1,969,537. August 7, 1934.

Electric translating system. 1,969,538. August 7, 1934.

Radioreceiver. 1,971,762. August 28, 1934.

Sound reproducing apparatus. 1,978,183. October 23, 1934.

Colored television apparatus. 1,988,931. January 22, 1935.

System of distribution. 1,993,581. March 5, 1935.

High frequency transmission system for railways. 2,001,514. May 14, 1935.

Torque amplifying system. 2,027,140. January 7, 1936.

Airplane landing field using directional radio beams. 2,077,196. April 13, 1937. [With J. H. Hammond, Jr.]

Electric valve converting system. Reissue 20,364. May 18, 1937.

Electric power system. 2,084,177. June 15, 1937. [With A. H. Mittag.]

Electric valve translating circuit. 2,092,545. September 7, 1937.

Electric translating circuit. 2,092,546. September 7, 1937.

Electric valve translating circuits. 2,098,023. November 2, 1937.

Electric valve circuits. 2,104,633. January 4, 1938.

Electric valve converting system. 2,122,271. June 28, 1938.

Discharge lamp system. 2,135,268. November 1, 1938.

Cable for transmitting electric power. 2,141,894. December 27, 1938.

Course guiding system. 2,184,267. December 26, 1939.

Protective system for electric valve translating apparatus. 2,186,815. January 9, 1940.

Electric valve circuit. 2,190,759. February 20, 1940.

Electric valve converting system. 2,193,912. March 19, 1940.

Electric valve frequency converting system. 2,193,913. March 19, 1940.

Electric valve frequency converting system. 2,193,914. March 19, 1940.

Asynchronous electric power transmission system. 2,207,570. July 9, 1940.

Electric power transmission system. 2,208,183. July 16, 1940.

Electric power transmission system. 2,213,945. September 10, 1940.

Excitation control system for synchronous machines. 2,215,312. September 17, 1940.

Electric valve converting system and control circuit therefor. 2,215,313. September 17, 1940.

Protective system. 2,222,696. November 26, 1940.

Electric power converting apparatus. 2,225,328. December 17, 1940.

Dynamoelectric machine. 2,227,992. January 7, 1941. [With M. A. Edwards.]

Electric motor control system. 2,236,984. April 1, 1941.

Electric power system. 2,237,384. April 8, 1941.

Frequency controlling system. 2,239,436. April 22, 1941.

Electric transforming apparatus. 2,240,201. April 29, 1941.

Navigation and landing of aircraft in fog. 2,245,246. June 10, 1941.

Radio distance meter. 2,248,599. July 8, 1941.

Electric valve circuits. 2,248,600. July 8, 1941. [With A. H. Mittag.]

Speed regulating system. 2,256,463. September 23, 1941.

Electric valve circuit. Reissue 21,919. October 14, 1941.

Radio distance meter. 2,259,982. October 21, 1941. [With F. G. Patterson and C. A. Nickle.]

Method of and apparatus for starting and operating thyratron motors. 2,262,482. November 11, 1941.

Electric motor control system. 2,285,182. June 2, 1942.

Electric drive. 2,312,061. February 23, 1943.

Electric drive. 2,312,062. February 23, 1943.

Electric drive. 2,315,489. April 6, 1943.

Electric drive. 2,315,490. April 6, 1943.

Electric drive. 2,315,491. April 6, 1943.

Speed control arrangement for induction clutches. 2,333,458. November 2, 1943.

Television system and operation. 2,333,969. November 9, 1943.

Control circuit for electric valve apparatus. 2,343,628. March 7, 1944.

Electric valve translating system. 2,357,067. August 29, 1944.

Electric ship propulsion system. 2,357,087. August 29, 1944.

Control system. 2,401,450. June 4, 1946.

Control system. 2,412,027. December 3, 1946.

Follow-up control system. 2,414,685. January 21, 1947. [With M. A. Edwards and K. K. Bowman.]

Follow-up control system. 2,414,919. January 28, 1947.

Follow-up system. 2,416,562. February 25, 1947.

Electric computer. 2,417,229. March 11, 1947.

Electric control circuits. 2,431,903. December 2, 1947. [With A. H. Mittag.]

High-frequency wave transmitting apparatus. 2,438,735. March 30, 1948.

Electric frequency transformation system. 2,451,189. October 12, 1948. [With A. H. Mittag and M. W. Sims.]

Radio landing apparatus. 2,451,793. October 19, 1948. [With F. G. Patterson.]

Pulse echo apparatus for spotting shellfire. 2,463,233. March 1, 1949.

Stabilizer for alternating current power transmission systems. 2,470,454. May 17, 1949.

Follow-up control system. 2,473,235. June 14, 1949. [With M. A. Edwards and G. A. Hoyt.]

Radio detection and ranging system employing multiple scan. 2,526,314. October 17, 1950.

Fault-suppressing circuits. 2,548,577. April 10, 1951. [With A. H. Mittag and E. L. Phillipi.]

Locomotive power system. 2,549,405. April 17, 1951. [With B. D. Bedford and A. H. Mittag.]

System for reproducing positions. 2,550,514. April 24, 1951.

Electronic frequency changer and stabilizing control means therefor. 2,586,498. February 19, 1952.

Current interrupter. 2,612,629. September 30, 1952. [With A. H. Mittag and R. W. Kuenning.]

Electric motor and stabilizing means therefor. 2,640,179. May 26, 1953. [With S. P. Nixdorff.]

Stabilizer for alternating current power transmission systems. 2,644,898. July 7, 1953. [With R. W. Kuenning.]

Electronic motor and commutating means therefor. 2,644,916. July 7, 1953. [With S. P. Nixdorff.]

Phase balancing system. 2,652,529. September 15, 1953.

Receiver for color television. 2,701,821. February 8, 1955.

Alternating-current motor. 2,707,257. April 26, 1955.

Alternating-current motor. 2,711,502. June 21, 1955.

Magnetic amplifier motor control. 2,752,549. June 26, 1956.

System for controlling the flow of molten metal. 2,768,413. October 30, 1956.

Alternating-current motor. 2,797,375. June 25, 1957.

Push-pull magnetic amplifier. 2,798,904. July 9, 1957.

Magnetic amplifier motor control system. 2,844,779. July 22, 1958.

Methods and systems for motor control. 2,851,647. September 9, 1958.

Motor control system. 2,876,408. March 3, 1959.

Magnetic computer. 2,984,414. May 16, 1961.

Electric motor control apparatus. 3,050,672. August 21, 1962.

Electric motor control apparatus. 3,082,367. March 19, 1963.

Electric motor control system. 3,119,957. January 28, 1964.

Adjustable speed motor control system. 3,736,481. May 29, 1973.

Title Index

Adjustable speed motor control system. 3,736,481.
Air-inlet valve for carbureters [sic]. 1,083,789.
Airplane landing field using directional radio beams. 2,077,196.
Alternating current commutator machine. 1,867,396.
Alternating-current-commutator motor. 1,194,923.
Alternating-current generator. 789,404; 789,476; 839,358.
Alternating-current high-frequency generator. 905,621.
Alternating-current motor. 841,610; 859,358; 873,702; 897,508; 923,753; 923,754; 927,398; 1,019,402; 1,060,731; 1,068,404; 1,194,265; 2,711,502; 2,797,375.
Alternating-current-motor control. 927,399; 946,751; 1,098,656; 1,603,102.
Amplifying electrical impulses. 1,906,441.
Amplifying system. 1,419,797.
Antenna. 1,360,167; 1,360,168; 1,677,698.

Apparatus for producing an electromotive force of special
wave form. 1,250,752.

Apparatus for producing and distributing electric-current
waves of radio frequency. 1,386,830.

Asynchronous electric power transmission system. 2,207,570.

Automatic control of phase-converters. 1,233,952.

Automatic control of phase-converters. Reissue 14,510.
August 27, 1918.

Automatic steering system. 1,958,258.

Bearing. 1,110,030; 1,315,069.

Boiler and heating arrangement therefor. 1,174,375.

Braking alternating-current motors. 967,295.

Cable for transmitting electric power. 2,141,894.

Circuit-control apparatus. 1,691,423.

Colored television apparatus. 1,988,931.

Commutator-motor. 949,992.

Compensated motor. 876,924.

Condenser. 1,266,377.

Control circuit for electric valve apparatus. 2,343,628.

Control of electric power. 1,655,036; 1,655,040; 1,719,866.

Control system. 1,461,571; 1,669,153; 1,787,299; 2,401,450;
2,412,027.

Controlling alternating currents. 1,206,643; 1,522,221;
1,634,970.

Cooling dynamo-electric machines. 1,382,878.

Course guiding system. 2,184,267.

Current interrupter. 2,612,629.

Discharge lamp system. 2,135,268.

Double-squirrel-cage synchronous motor. 1,495,969.

Dynamo-electric machine. 849,713; 861,072; 949,345;
1,091,613; 1,091,614; 1,092,420; 2,227,992.

Electric apparatus. 1,694,244.

Electric braking. 967,296; 974,224.

Electric braking with alternating-current motors. 1,089,384.

Electric computer. 2,417,229.

Electric control circuits. 2,431,903.

Electric discharge device. 1,787,300.
Electric drive. 2,312,061; 2,312,062; 2,315,489; 2,315,490;
    2,315,491.
Electric frequency transformation system. 2,451,189.
Electric locomotive. 949,347.
Electric motor. 919,514; 923,311; 1,667,647.
Electric motor and stabilizing means therefor. 2,640,179.
Electric motor control apparatus. 3,050,672; 3,082,367.
Electric motor control system. 2,236,984; 2,285,182;
    3,119,957.
Electric power converting apparatus. 2,225,328.
Electric power system. 2,084,177; 2,237,384.
Electric power transmission system. 2,208,183; 2,213,945.
Electric ship propulsion. 1,481,853; 1,481,882; 1,579,051;
    1,701,350.
Electric ship propulsion system. 2,357,087.
Electric system of ship propulsion. 1,304,240.
Electric transforming apparatus. 2,240,201.
Electric translating circuit. 2,092,546.
Electric translating system. 1,969,538; 2,357,067.
Electric valve circuit. 2,190,759.
Electric valve circuit. Reissue 21,919. October 14, 1941.
Electric valve circuits. 2,104,633; 2,248,600.
Electric valve converting system. 1,937,377; 1,939,428;
    1,939,429; 2,122,271; 2,193,912.
Electric valve converting system. Reissue 20,364. May 18,
    1937.
Electric valve converting system and control circuit therefor.
    2,215,313.
Electric valve excitation circuits. 1,954,661.
Electric valve frequency converting system. 2,193,913;
    2,193,914.
Electric valve translating circuit. 2,092,545.
Electric valve translating circuits. 2,098,023.
Electrical system. 1,896,534.
Electrical system of power transmission. 1,268,662;
    1,304,239.

Electrical transmission of pictures. 1,694,301.
Electrical transmission system. 1,921,718.
Electron-discharge device. 1,535,082.
Electronic frequency changer and stabilizing control means
    therefor. 2,586,498.
Electronic motor and commutating means therefor. 2,644,916.
Eliminating fading. 1,853,021.
Excitation control system for synchronous machines.
    2,215,312.
Fault-suppressing circuits. 2,548,577.
Follow-up control system. 2,414,685; 2,414,919; 2,473,235.
Follow-up system. 2,416,562.
Frequency-changer. 859,359.
Frequency controlling system. 2,239,436.
Frequency transformation. 1,174,793.
Ground-detector and cut-out. 825,286.
High-frequency alternator. 1,008,577; 1,110,028; 1,110,029;
    1,126,334; 1,229,856; 1,366,627; 1,369,601; 1,426,943.
High-frequency signaling system. 1,466,263; 1,500,785;
    1,610,073; 1,648,711.
High frequency transmission system for railways. 2,001,514.
High-frequency wave transmitting apparatus. 2,438,735.
High-speed rotating body. 1,208,441.
Ignition system. 1,723,908.
Indicating altitude from aircraft. 1,913,148.
Indicating system for aircraft. 1,907,471.
Induction-generator. 920,809.
Induction-motor. 872,550; 1,119,741; 1,185,461.
Induction-motor control. 882,606; 901,513.
Internal-combustion hydraulic pump. 1,259,338.
Locomotive control. 1,655,037.
Locomotive power system. 2,549,405.
Magnetic amplifier motor control. 2,752,549.
Magnetic amplifier motor control system. 2,844,779.
Magnetic computer. 2,984,414.

Manufacturing rotating bodies for high-speed machinery.
998,734.

Means for compensating polyphase alternating-current
commutation-motors. 1,080,403.

Means for controlling alternating currents. 1,328,473;
1,328,797; 1,334,126.

Means for controlling self-exciting generators. 829,133.

Means for frequency transformations. 1,382,877.

Method and apparatus for picture transmission by wire or
radio. 1,787,851.

Method and means for determining altitude from aircraft.
1,969,537.

Method of and apparatus for indicating the speed of electric
motors. 1,100,280.

Method of and apparatus for multiplex signaling. 1,771,700.

Method of and apparatus for relaying high-frequency currents.
1,042,069.

Method of and apparatus for starting and operating thyratron
motors. 2,262,482.

Method of and means for controlling electrical energy.
1,340,101.

Method of and means for controlling high-frequency
alternating currents. 1,328,610.

Methods and systems for motor control. 2,851,647.

Motor control. 885,128; 936,071; 957,454; 996,390.

Motor-control system. 940,112; 1,280,624; 2,876,408.

Motor excitation. 1,289,592.

Motor-winding. 841,609.

Multispeed alternating-current motor. 1,263,992.

Navigation and landing of aircraft in fog. 2,245,246.

Neutralizing inductive disturbances. 1,120,992.

Operating electric motors. 1,563,004.

Oscillation generator. 1,698,290.

Overload protective device. 954,845.

Phase-balancer. 1,093,594.

Phase-balancer. Reissue 14,133. May 16, 1916.

Phase balancing system. 2,652,529.
Picture transmission. 1,857,130.
Picture transmission apparatus. 1,866,338.
Power-amplifying means. 1,706,094.
Power-factor control system. 1,655,038.
Power-transmitting mechanism. 1,223,924.
Protective means for alternating-current systems. 819,627.
Protective system. 2,222,696.
Protective system for electric valve translating apparatus.
    2,186,815.
Pulse echo apparatus for spotting shellfire. 2,463,233.
Push-pull magnetic amplifier. 2,798,904.
Radiant energy guiding system for airplanes. 1,917,114.
Radio detection and ranging system employing multiple scan.
    2,526,314.
Radio distance meter. 2,248,599; 2,259,982.
Radio landing apparatus. 2,451,793.
Radioreceiver. 1,971,762.
Radio receiving system. 1,350,912; 1,373,931; 1,375,992;
    1,477,413; 1,491,372; 1,546,878; 1,723,907.
Radio signaling system. 1,320,959; 1,360,169; 1,426,944;
    1,564,807; 1,775,801; 1,790,646; 1,797,039; 1,814,813.
Radiotelegraphy. 1,768,433.
Radio transmitting system. 1,517,816.
Receiver for color television. 2,701,821.
Rectifying apparatus. 1,718,515.
Regenerative electric regulator. 1,917,146.
Regulating apparatus. 1,655,041.
Regulating system. 1,655,035.
Regulating system for alternating-current circuits. 1,337,875.
Regulator for phase-balancers. 1,233,953.
Reinforcer for telephone-circuits. 996,391.
Removing sleet from antennae. 1,404,726.
Rotary transforming apparatus. 1,420,398.
Rotor for dynamo-electric machines. 1,261,673.
Selective tuning system. 1,173,079.

Self-excited alternator. 881,647.

Self-exciting generator. 895,933.

Series-multiple control. 1,300,542; 1,365,441.

Signaling. 1,839,455.

Signaling by phase displacement. 1,882,698.

Signaling system. 1,549,737; 1,722,998.

Single-phase commutator-motor. 951,357; 953,366.

Single-phase motor. 920,710; 935,881; 1,021,289.

Single-phase-motor control. 923,312; 927,397; 949;346.

Sound-motion picture producer. 1,937,378.

Sound reproducing apparatus. 1,978,183.

Speed control arrangement for induction clutches. 2,333,458.

Speed control of induction-motors. 1,301,632.

Speed-control system. 1,655,039; 1,655,042; 1,736,689.

Speed-indicating system. 1,747,041.

Speed regulating system. 2,256,463.

Split-phase system. 1,170,211.

Stabilization of tuned radio frequency amplifiers. 1,775,544.

Stabilizer for alternating current power transmission systems.
     2,470,454; 2,644,898.

Starting motor-converter. 876,923.

Starting phase-converters. 1,300,545.

Surge preventer. 1,554,698.

Synchronous motor. 785,532; 897,507.

System for controlling the flow of molten metal. 2,768,413.

System for producing high frequency oscillations. 1,866,337.

System for reproducing positions. 2,550,514.

System of distribution. 1,537,055; 1,620,506; 1,680,758;
     1,800,002; 1,835,131; 1,993,581.

System of electric distribution. 921,786.

System of electric power transmission. 1,917,081; 1,917,082.

System of electric ship propulsion. 1,289,593; 1,676,312.

System of electrical distribution. 1,150,652; 1,242,632;
     1,375,991; 1,677,699; 1,677,700.

System of frequency transformation. 1,316,995.

System of motor control. 1,490,720.

System of phase modification. 1,300,543; 1,300,544.
System of radio communication. 1,400,847.
System of ship propulsion. 1,215,094; 1,215,095; 1,723,906.
Telephone-relay. 902,195.
Telephone relay and system. 996,445.
Telephone system. 1,102,628.
Television apparatus. 1,935,427.
Television receiver. 1,889,587.
Television system and operation. 2,333,969.
Torque amplifying system. 2,027,140.
Transmission of pictures. 1,694,302; 1,752,876; 1,783,031;
   1,792,264; 1,830,586.
Transmitting angular motion. 1,600,204.
Two-speed winding for three-phase motors. 785,533.
Unidirectional radio receiving system. 1,465,108.
Voltage-regulator. 805,253; 829,826; 1,652,923.
Winding for three-phase motors. 785,995.
Wireless signaling system. 1,313,042; 1,350,911; 1,465,961;
   1,465,962; 1,501,830; 1,508,151.
Wireless-telephone system. 1,313,041.

EDWIN ARMSTRONG (1890-1954)

Wireless receiving system. 1,113,149. October 6, 1914.
207:254.

Electric-wave transmission. 1,334,165. March 16, 1920.
272:489. [With Michael I. Pupin.]

Antenna with distributed positive resistance. 1,336,378. April
6, 1920. 273:127. [With Michael I. Pupin.]

Receiving high-frequency oscillations. 1,342,885. June 8,
1920. 275:303.

Multiple antenna for electrical wave transmission. 1,388,441.
August 23, 1921. 289:674. [With Michael I. Pupin.]

Selectively opposing impedance to received electrical
oscillations. 1,415,845. May 9, 1922. [With Michael I.
Pupin.]

Radioreceiving system having high selectivity. 1,416,061.
May 16, 1922. [With Michael I. Pupin.]

Tone-producing radioreceiver. 1,502,875. July 29, 1924.
[With Michael I. Pupin.]

Wave signaling system. 1,539,820. June 2, 1925.

Wave signaling system. 1,539,821. June 2, 1925.

Wave signaling system. 1,539,822. June 2, 1925.

Wave signaling system. 1,541,780. June 16, 1925.

Wave-signaling system. 1,545,724. July 14, 1925.

Wireless receiving system for continuous waves. 1,611,848. December 21, 1926.

Wave signaling system. 1,675,323. July 3, 1928.

Wave signaling system. 1,716,573. June 11, 1929.

Radio signaling system. 1,941,066. December 26, 1933.

Radio broadcasting and receiving. 1,941,067. December 26, 1933.

Radiosignaling. 1,941,068. December 26, 1933.

Radiosignaling. 1,941,069. December 26, 1933.

Radiotelephone signaling. 1,941,447. December 26, 1933.

Radio signaling system. 2,024,138. December 17, 1935.

Radio transmitting system. 2,063,074. December 8, 1936.

Radio signaling system. 2,082,935. June 8, 1937.

Radio transmitting system. 2,098,698. November 9, 1937.

Radio signaling system. 2,104,011. January 4, 1938.

Multiplex radio signaling system. 2,104,012. January 4, 1938.

Radio receiving system. 2,116,501. May 10, 1938.

Radio receiving system. 2,116,502. May 10, 1938.

Frequency changing system. 2,122,401. July 5, 1938.

Radio transmitting system. 2,130,172. September 13, 1938.

Radio transmitting system. 2,169,212. August 15, 1939.

Radio transmitting system. 2,203,712. June 11, 1940.

Frequency modulation signaling system. 2,215,284. September 17, 1940.

Frequency modulation signaling system. Reissue 21,660. December 17, 1940.

Relaying frequency modulated signals. 2,264,608. December 2, 1941.

Relaying frequency modulated signals. 2,275,486. March 10, 1942.

Radio rebroadcasting system. 2,276,008. March 10, 1942.

Frequency modulation system. 2,290,159. July 21, 1942.

Current limiting device. 2,295,323. September 8, 1942.

Method and means for transmitting frequency modulated signals. 2,315,308. March 30, 1943.

Receiving radio signals. 2,318,137. May 4, 1943.

Frequency modulation signaling system. 2,323,698. July 6, 1943.

Frequency-modulated carrier signal receiver. 2,540,643. February 6, 1951.

Radio signaling. 2,602,885. July 18, 1952.

Frequency modulation multiplex system. 2,630,497. March 3, 1953.

Radio detection and ranging systems. 2,738,502. March 13, 1956. [Edwin H. Armstrong, deceased (E. M. Armstrong, executrix), J. H. Bose, and R. E. Hull.]

Multiplex frequency modulation transmitter. 2,773,125. December 4, 1956. [Edwin H. Armstrong, deceased (E. M. Armstrong, executrix).]

Linear detector for subcarrier frequency modulated waves. 2,835,803. May 20, 1958. [John H. Bose to E. M. Armstrong, executrix.]

Noise reduction in phase shift modulation. 2,871,292. January 27, 1959. [John H. Bose to E. M. Armstrong, executrix of the estate of E. H. Armstrong.]

Stabilized multiple frequency modulation receiver. 2,879,335. March 24, 1959. [John H. Bose to E. M. Armstrong, executrix of the estate of E. H. Armstrong.]

Title Index

Electric-wave transmission. 1,334,165.
Frequency changing system. 2,122,401.
Frequency-modulated carrier signal receiver. 2,540,643.
Frequency modulation multiplex system. 2,630,497.
Frequency modulation signaling system. 2,215,284;
     2,323,698.
Frequency modulation signaling system. Reissue 21,660.
     December 17, 1940.
Frequency modulation system. 2,290,159.
Linear detector for subcarrier frequency modulated waves.
     2,835,803.
Method and means for transmitting frequency modulated
     signals. 2,315,308.
Multiple antenna for electrical wave transmission. 1,388,441.
Multiplex frequency modulation transmitter. 2,773,125.
Multiplex radio signaling system. 2,104,012.
Noise reduction in phase shift modulation. 2,871,292.
Radio broadcasting and receiving. 1,941,066.
Radio detection and ranging systems. 2,738,502.
Radio transmitting system. 2,169,212.
Radio rebroadcasting system. 2,276,008.
Radio receiving system. 2,116,501; 2,116,502.
Radio signaling. 2,602,885.
Radio signaling system. 1,941,066; 2,024,138; 2,082,935;
     2,104,011.
Radio transmitting system. 2,063,074; 2,098,698; 2,130,172;
     2,203,712.
Radioreceiving system having high selectivity. 1,416,061.
Radiosignaling. 1,941,068; 1,941,069.
Radiotelephone signaling. 1,941,447.
Receiving high-frequency oscillations. 1,342,885.
Receiving radio signals. 2,318,137.
Regeneration. *See* 1,113,149.
Relaying frequency modulated signals. 2,264,608; 2,275,486.
Selectively opposing impedance to received electrical
     oscillations. 1,415,845.

Stabilized multiple frequency modulation receiver. 2,879,335.
Superheterodyne. *See* 1,342,885.
Superregeneration. *See* 1,416,061.
Tone-producing radioreceiver. 1,502,875.
Wave signaling system. 1,539,820; 1,539,821; 1,539,822;
    1,541,789; 1,545,724; 1,675,323; 1,716,573.
Wireless receiving system. 1,113,149.
Wireless receiving system for continuous waves. 1,611,848.

HOLLIS BAIRD (1906-1990)

Short wave reception. 1,816,461. July 28, 1931.

Signal amplifying system and method. 1,816,462. July 28, 1931.

Scanning apparatus for television. 1,908,809. May 16, 1933.

Scanning device for television. 1,962,474. June 12, 1934.

Television. 2,050,149. August 4, 1936.

JOHN L. BAIRD (1888-1946)

Light-sensitive electric device. 1,697,451. January 1, 1929.

Apparatus for transmitting views or images to a distance. 1,699,270. January 15, 1929.

Television apparatus. 1,707,935. April 2, 1929.

Television and like system. 1,735,946. November 19, 1929.

Facsimile telegraphy. 1,757,352. May 6, 1930.

Recording of views of objects or scenes or optical images or the like. 1,776,097. September 16, 1930.

Television or like system and apparatus. 1,781,210. November 11, 1930.

Transmitting signals. 1,781,799. November 18, 1930.

Transmitting apparatus and the like. 1,781,800. November 18, 1930.

Apparatus for producing a varying light or illumination. 1,800,044. April 7, 1931.

Glow-discharge lamp. 1,800,926. April 14, 1931.

Television and like apparatus. 1,807,464. May 26, 1931.

Television and like apparatus. 1,807,465. May 26, 1931.

Driving television or other apparatus at a predetermined speed. 1,816,106. July 28, 1931.

Television and like apparatus. 1,869,735. August 2, 1932.

Television or like system and apparatus. 1,890,558. December 13, 1932.

Exploring device for television apparatus. 1,913,911. June 13, 1933.

Television apparatus and the like. 1,925,554. September 5, 1933.

Television system. 1,945,626. February 6, 1934.

Television apparatus. 1,957,815. May 8, 1934.

Transmitting signals. Reissue 19,169. May 15, 1934.

Television and like apparatus. 1,980,150. November 6, 1934.

Television apparatus. 2,006,124. June 25, 1935.

Cinematographic rectifying system. 2,032,164. February 25, 1936.

Television and like apparatus. 2,056,761. October 6, 1936.

Method of and apparatus for producing images by television in stereoscopic relief. 2,349,071. May 16, 1944.

Screen for television. 2,425,980. August 19, 1947. [With K. E. Shelley.]

Title Index

Apparatus for producing a varying light or illumination. 1,800,044.

Apparatus for transmitting views or images to a distance. 1,699,270.

Cinematographic rectifying system. 2,032,164.

Driving television or other apparatus at a predetermined speed. 1,816,106.

Exploring device for television apparatus. 1,913,911.

Facsimile telegraphy. 1,757,352.

Glow-discharge lamp. 1,800,926.

Light-sensitive electric device. 1,697,451.

Method of and apparatus for producing images by television in stereoscopic relief. 2,349,071.

Recording of views of objects or scenes or optical images or the like. 1,776,097.

Screen for television. 2,425,980.

Television and like apparatus. 1,807,464; 1,807,465; 1,869,735; 1,980,150; 2,056,761.

Television and like system. 1,735,946.

Television apparatus. 1,707,935; 1,957,815; 2,006,124.

Television apparatus and the like. 1,925,554.

Television or like system and apparatus. 1,781,210; 1,890,558.

Television system. 1,945,626.

Transmitting apparatus and the like. 1,781,800.

Transmitting signals. 1,781,799.

Transmitting signals. Reissue 19,169. May 15, 1934.

JOHN RENSHAW CARSON (1866-1940)

Duplex wireless system. 1,188,531. June 27, 1916. 227:1171.

Method of and means for transmitting signals. 1,243,705. October 23, 1917. 243:808.

Wireless receiving system. 1,244,697. October 30, 1917. 243:1149.

Wireless signaling system. 1,309,459. July 8, 1919. 264:296.

Wireless system. 1,309,538. July 8, 1919. 264:311. [With John Mills.]

Translating-circuits. 1,312,433. August 5, 1919. 265:109.

Distortion-correcting circuit. 1,315,539. September 9, 1919. 266:204.

Duplex translating circuits. 1,343,306. June 15, 1920. 275:448.

Duplex translating circuits. 1,343,307. June 15, 1920. 275:448.

Duplex translating circuits. 1,343,308. June 15, 1920. 275:448.

Frequency-control system. 1,403,841. January 17, 1922.

Method of and means for modulating carrier oscillations. 1,410,890. March 28, 1922.

Translating circuits. 1,448,702. March 13, 1923.

Method and means for signaling with high-frequency waves. 1,449,382. March 27, 1923.

Receiving circuits for weak signal currents. 1,450,969. April 10, 1923.

Translating circuits. 1,463,795. August 7, 1923.

Translating circuits. 1,463,796. August 7, 1923.

Signaling system. 1,516,518. November 25, 1924.

Receiving weak signal currents. 1,532,172. April 7, 1925.

Telegraph signaling system. 1,559,159. October 27, 1925.

Loading system. 1,564,201. December 8, 1925. [With A. B. Clark and John Mills.]

Translating circuit. 1,672,056. June 5, 1928.

Concentric conductor transmission system. 1,817,964. August 11, 1931. [With S. P. Mead.]

Title Index

Concentric conductor transmission system. 1,817,964.

Distortion-correcting circuit. 1,315,539.

Duplex translating circuits. 1,343,306; 1,343,307; 1,343,308.

Duplex wireless system. 1,188,531.

Frequency-control system. 1,403,841.

Loading system. 1,564,201.

Method and means for signaling with high-frequency waves. 1,449,382.

Method of and means for modulating carrier oscillations. 1,410,890.

Method of and means for transmitting signals. 1,243,705.

Receiving circuits for weak signal currents. 1,450,969.

Receiving weak signal currents. 1,532,172.

Signaling system. 1,516,518.

Single side band. *See* 1,449,382.

Telegraph signaling system. 1,559,159.

Translating circuit. 1,672,056.

Translating circuits. 1,312,433; 1,448,702; 1,463,795; 1,463,796.

Wireless receiving system. 1,244,697.

Wireless signaling system. 1,309,459.

Wireless system. 1,309,538.

EDWIN H. COLPITTS (1872-1949)

Magnetic core for inductance coils. 705,935. July 29, 1902. 100:1078. [With John C. Lee.]

Composite transmission over loaded electric circuits. 712,766. November 4, 1902. 101:1010.

Connecting circuit for magneto telephone-exchange systems. 1,029,593. June 18, 1912. 179:587.

Electromagnetic coil. 1,116,020. November 3, 1914. 208:190.

Electric wave-amplifier. 1,128,292. February 16, 1915. 211:662.

System for amplifying electric waves. 1,129,959. March 2, 1915. 212:43.

System for the transmission of intelligence. 1,137,384. April 27, 1915. 213:1294.

System for measuring capacities. 1,167,677. January 11, 1916. 222:495. [With George A. Campbell and O. B. Blackwell.]

Multiplex radiotelegraph system. 1,194,820. August 15, 1916. 229:786.

Control device for wireless signaling. 1,198,699. September 19, 1916. 230:768.

Control device for wireless signaling. 1,198,700. September 19, 1916. 230:769.

Telephone transmission system. 1,200,082. October 3, 1916. 231:117.

System for the transmission of intelligence. Reissue 14,380. October 23, 1917. 243:1037.

Wireless telegraphy and telephony. 1,256,983. February 19, 1918. 247:624.

Signaling method and system. 1,375,675. April 26, 1921. 285:579.

Transmission of intelligence. 1,388,450. August 23, 1921. 289:676.

Control device for wireless signaling. Reissue 15,538. February 13, 1923.

High-frequency signaling. 1,452,957. April 24, 1923.

Multiplex radiotelegraph system. 1,465,932. August 28, 1923.

Multiplex signaling system. 1,472,585. October 30, 1923.

Method of and apparatus for recording sound. 1,540,317. June 2, 1925. [With Edward B. Craft.]

Carrier-wave transmission. 1,573,303. February 16, 1926.

Oscillation generator. 1,624,537. April 12, 1927.

Title Index

Carrier-wave transmission. 1,573,303.
Colpitts oscillator. *See* 1,624,537.
Composite transmission over loaded electric circuits. 712,766.
Connecting circuit for magneto telephone-exchange systems.
1,029,593.
Control device for wireless signaling. 1,198,699; 1,198,700.
Control device for wireless signaling. Reissue 15,538.
February 13, 1923.
Electric wave-amplifier. 1,128,292.
Electromagnetic coil. 1,116,020.
High-frequency signaling. 1,452,957.
Magnetic core for inductance coils. 705,935.
Method of and apparatus for recording sound. 1,540,317.
Multiplex radiotelegraph system. 1,194,820; 1,465,932.
Multiplex signaling system. 1,472,585.
Oscillation generator. 1,624,537.
Signaling method and system. 1,375,675.
System for amplifying electric waves. 1,129,959.
System for measuring capacities. 1,167,677.
System for the transmission of intelligence. 1,137,384.
System for the transmission of intelligence. Reissue 14,380.
October 23, 1917.
Telephone transmission system. 1,200,082.
Transmission of intelligence. 1,388,450.
Wireless telegraphy and telephony. 1,256,983.

FRANK CONRAD (1874-1941)

Electric-arc lamp. 599,931. March 1, 1898. 82:1305. [With Harry P. Davis.]

Electric meter and motor. 608,842. August 9, 1898. 84:914. [With Harry P. Davis.]

Alternating-current-measuring equipment. 611,466. September 27, 1898. 84:1962. [With Harry P. Davis.]

Alternating-current voltmeter. 611,592. September 27, 1898. 84:2007. [With Harry P. Davis.]

Electrical measuring instrument. 627,908. June 27, 1899. [With Harry P. Davis.]

Electrical measuring instrument. 629,663. July 25, 1899. 88:673. [With Harry P. Davis.]

Instrument for indicating the phase and frequency relations of alternating currents. 695,913. March 25, 1902. 98:2375.

Means for measuring the energy of three-phase alternating-current circuits. 716,867. December 30, 1902. 101:2834.

Ground-detector for electric circuits. 716,868. December 30, 1902. 101:2835.

Measuring the energy of three-phase alternating-current circuits. 717,496. December 30, 1902. 101:3084.

Prepayment electrical measuring device. 757,439. April 19, 1904. 109:1897.

Alternating-current wattmeter. 760,426. May 24, 1904. 110:87.

Circuit making and breaking relay. 780,024. January 17, 1905. 114:551.

Constant current regulator. 792,120. June 13, 1905. 116:1796.

Electrical measuring instrument. 794,395. July 11, 1905. 117:400.

Measuring instrument. 798,167. August 29, 1905. 117:2414.

Spring-abutment for measuring instruments. 798,168. August 29, 1905. 117:2415.

Switch for electric circuits. 803,212. October 31, 1905. 118:2358. [With Arthur B. Reynders.]

Alternating-current system of control. 803,213. October 31, 1905. 118:2359.

Regulating means for systems of electrical distribution. 807,943. December 19, 1905. 119:2152. [With B. G. Lamme and C. F. Scott.]

Transformer. 829,572. August 28, 1906. 123:2740.

Protective apparatus for electrical circuits. 840,478. January 8, 1907. 126:404. [With Harry P. Davis.]

Protective apparatus for parallel transmission-lines. 840,479. January 8, 1907. 126:404. [With Harry P. Davis.]

Transformer. 841,076. January 8, 1907. 126:700.

Alternating-current electrical apparatus. 853,226. May 14, 1907. 128:472. [With William M. Bradshaw.]

Automatic synchronizer. 885,143. April 21, 1908. 133:1732.

Electric heating apparatus. 912,994. February 23, 1909. 139:740.

Voltage-regulator. 923,627. June 1, 1909. 143:176.

System for vapor electric apparatus. 931,114. August 17, 1909. 145:549.

System of distribution for mercury-vapor rectifiers. 931,115. August 17, 1909. 145:550.

Overload and reverse current relay device. 933,746. September 14, 1909. 146:266.

Overload and reverse current relay device. 934,390. September 14, 1909. 146:478.

Overload and reverse current relay device. 934,391. September 14, 1909. 146:478.

Electrical system. 934,596. September 21, 1909. 146:569.

Armature-winding. 954,614. April 12, 1910. 153:348.

Mercury-vapor rectifier. 969,525. September 6, 1910. 158:125.

Starting means for vapor-rectifying devices. 975,399. November 15, 1910. 160:504.

Carbureter [sic]. 1,002,646. September 5, 1911. 170:154.

Transformer. 1,005,163. October 10, 1911. 171:235.

Prepayment-meter. 1,017,082. February 13, 1912. 175:329.

System of electric-motor control. 1,024,557. April 30, 1912. 177:1075.

Metering system. 1,029,743. June 18, 1912. 179:642.

Recording measuring instrument. 1,031,041. July 2, 1912. 180:67.

Recording measuring instrument. 1,031,042. July 2, 1912. 180:68.

Wattmeter. 1,067,311. July 15, 1913. 192:553.

Impedance device for use with current-rectifiers. 1,075,404. October 14, 1913. 195:309. [With Y. Sakai.]

Vapor electric device. 1,101,523. June 30, 1914. 203:1269.

Electrical apparatus. 1,106,368. August 11, 1914. 205:314.

System of distribution. 1,108,886. September 1, 1914. 206:7.

Current-rectifying device. 1,112,265. September 29, 1914. 206:1356.

Rectifier system. 1,112,266. September 29, 1914. 206:1357.

System of electrical distribution and regulation. 1,112,438. October 6, 1914. 207:8.

Electrical regulator. 1,122,693. December 29, 1914. 209:1478.

Transformer for use with current-rectifying apparatus. 1,123,248. January 5, 1915. 210:16.

Safety device for starting motors. 1,130,573. March 2, 1915. 212:257.

Overload and reverse current relay. 1,137,840. May 4, 1915. 214:41.

System of electrical distribution. 1,138,637. May 11, 1915. 214:358. [With Harry P. Davis.]

Electric measuring instrument. 1,141,380. June 1, 1915. 215:106.

Storage-battery regulator. 1,146,924. July 20, 1915. 216:722.

Electrical regulator. 1,146,925. July 20, 1915. 216:722.

Regulator for electrical circuits. 1,146,926. July 20, 1915. 216:723.

Electrical regulator. 1,146,927. July 20, 1915. 216:723.

Pressure-gage. 1,150,016. August 17, 1915. 217:712.

Protective means for electrical systems. 1,155,133. September 28, 1915. 218:1068.

Means for protecting electrical systems. 1,155,134. September 28, 1915. 218:1069.

Electrically operated device. 1,158,898. November 2, 1915. 220:171.

Vapor electric device. 1,159,900. November 9, 1915. 220:557.

System of electrical distribution. 1,159,904. November 9, 1915. 220:558. [With Harry P. Davis.]

Starting means for vapor electric devices. 1,166,186. December 28, 1915. 221:1333.

Gear-wheel. 1,167,742. January 11, 1916. 222:516.

Gear. 1,167,743. January 11, 1916. 222:517.

Spark-advancer. 1,171,594. February 15, 1916. 223:721.

Vehicle-lighting system. 1,171,595. February 15, 1916. 223:721.

Interrupter. 1,171,596. February 15, 1916. 223:721.

Starting mechanism for automobiles. 1,175,342. March 14, 1916. 224:505.

Plug-connector. 1,175,343. March 14, 1916. 224:505.

Electrical system. 1,191,158. July 18, 1916. 228:774.

Starting-electrode for vapor electric devices. 1,194,143. August 8, 1916. 229:505.

Vapor-rectifier. 1,204,411. November 14, 1916. 232:333.

Starting mechanism for automobiles. 1,215,490. February 13, 1917. 235:386. [With J. P. Nikonow.]

Ignition system. 1,219,704. March 20, 1917. 236:699.

System of electrical distribution. 1,224,143. May 1, 1917. 238:10.

Cut-out. 1,229,719. June 12, 1917. 239:502.

Vapor current-rectifying device. 1,234,875. July 31, 1917. 240:1225.

Electrical system. 1,234,876. July 31, 1917. 240:1225.

Electrical system. 1,235,012. July 31, 1917. 240:1270.

Starting and ignition machine. 1,237,172. August 14, 1917. 241:560.

Electrical system. 1,246,056. November 13, 1917. 244:303.

Starting mechanism for automobiles. 1,246,057. November 13, 1917. 244:304.

Starting system for automobiles. 1,246,717. November 13, 1917. 244:500.

Starting motor for gas-engines. 1,246,718. November 13, 1917. 244:500.

Ignition mechanism. 1,248,459. December 4, 1917. 245:9.

Electrical system for automobiles. 1,248,460. December 4, 1917. 245:9.

Regulator and cut-out. 1,260,647. March 26, 1918. 248:883.

Electrical system. 1,260,648. March 26, 1918. 248:884.

Regulator and cut-out. 1,260,649. March 26, 1918. 248:884.

Vapor-arc rectifier. 1,264,276. April 30, 1918. 249:1031.

Priming device for internal-combustion engines. 1,271,670. July 9, 1918. 252:290.

Starting system for automobiles. 1,274,992. August 6, 1918. 253:185.

Ignition mechanism. 1,277,388. September 3, 1918. 254:16.

Vapor electric apparatus. 1,285,947. November 26, 1918. 256:749.

Side lamp for automobiles. 1,296,482. March 4, 1919. 260:148.

Gear-shifting mechanism. 1,296,483. March 4, 1919. 260:148.

Hand-grenade. 1,304,544. May 27, 1919. 262:492.

Radiotelegraphy system. 1,314,789. September 2, 1919. 266:59.

Starting mechanism for gas-engines. 1,317,269. September 30, 1919. 266:625.

Connector. 1,318,728. October 14, 1919. 267:265.

System of electrical distribution. 1,320,083. October 28, 1919. 267:570. [With Charles M. Moss, F. C. Hanker, and H. A. Travers.]

Ignition system. 1,338,360. April 27, 1920. 273:708. [With J. S. Kinney.]

Mounting for oil-pumps. 1,344,756. June 29, 1920. 275:863.

Ignition system. 1,352,431. September 14, 1920. 278:173.

Electrical ignition system. 1,352,432. September 14, 1920. 278:173.

Electrical ignition system. 1,352,433. September 14, 1920. 278:173.

Ignition system. 1,352,434. September 14, 1920. 278:173.

Gear-shift mechanism. 1,363,719. December 28, 1920. 281:677.

Starting mechanism for gas engines. 1,370,005. March 1, 1921. 284:48.

Starting mechanism for automobiles. 1,385,983. August 2, 1921. 289:4.

Starting mechanism for internal-combustion engines. 1,413,829. April 25, 1922.

Distributor for ignition apparatus. 1,417,717. May 30, 1922.

Apparatus for the receipt of wireless impulses. 1,456,867. May 29, 1923.

Spark-advancing mechanism. 1,466,272. August 28, 1923.

Radiomodulation system. 1,477,316. December 11, 1923.

Tuning system of antennae. 1,502,848. July 29, 1924.

Receiving circuit for the elimination of static disturbances. 1,513,223. October 28, 1924.

Aperiodic receiver system. 1,515,186. November 11, 1924.

Wireless telephone system. 1,528,047. March 3, 1925.

Regulator system. 1,543,696. June 30, 1925.

Signaling system. 1,563,342. December 1, 1925.

Volt-ampere meter. 1,571,234. February 2, 1926.

Wireless transmission system. 1,586,653. June 1, 1926.

Inductance device. 1,635,541. July 12, 1927.

Wireless antenna system. 1,640,534. August 30, 1927.

Polyphase plate-circuit excitation system. 1,645,291. October 11, 1927. [With A. Nyman.]

Radio transmitting system. 1,652,516. December 13, 1927.

Radio sending system. 1,654,322. December 27, 1927.

Wireless receiving cabinet. 1,655,985. January 10, 1928.

Telephone device. 1,660,864. February 28, 1928.

Wireless receiving set. 1,664,192. March 27, 1928.

Telephone device. 1,680,409. August 14, 1928.

Directive antenna system. 1,689,863. October 30, 1928.

Aerial system. 1,691,338. November 13, 1928.

Telephone circuits and apparatus. 1,693,401. November 27, 1928. [With A. Nyman.]

Electrical measuring instrument. 1,695,917. December 18, 1928.

Inductor helix. 1,702,461. February 19, 1929.

Multiple electrode vacuum tube. 1,709,659. April 16, 1929.

Insulator. 1,730,124. October 1, 1929.

Duplex radio transmission system. 1,732,741. October 22, 1929.

Antenna system. 1,750,347. March 11, 1930.

Short-wave antenna. 1,768,666. July 1, 1930.

Frequency-control device. 1,768,888. July 1, 1930. [With John B. Coleman.]

Modulation system. 1,799,974. April 7, 1931.

Telephone receiver. 1,819,499. August 18, 1931.

Condenser. 1,837,017. December 15, 1931.

Television system. 1,853,661. April 12, 1932.

Constant frequency generator. 1,872,896. August 23, 1932.

Radio relay system. 1,877,815. September 20, 1932.

Electric clock. 1,911,062. May 23, 1933.

Control device. 1,934,524. November 7, 1933.

Motion-picture apparatus. 1,939,031. December 12, 1933.
[With Christian Aalborg.]

Transmission system. 1,939,042. December 12, 1933.

Refrigerator. 1,982,375. November 27, 1934. [With Christian Aalborg.]

Television apparatus. 1,991,082. February 12, 1935.

Motion picture apparatus. 2,023,065. December 3, 1935.

Motion picture apparatus. 2,032,116. February 25, 1936.
[With C. Aalborg, O. B. French, and N. J. Collingswood.]

Refrigerator apparatus. 2,056,646. October 6, 1936.

Radio communication system. 2,057,640. October 13, 1936.

Battery-charging system. 2,117,018. May 10, 1938. [With
G. C. Goode.]

Double-winding generator and rectifier combination.
2,117,019. May 10, 1938.

Copper-oxide rectifier. 2,117,020. May 10, 1938.

Time switch. 2,121,585. June 21, 1938.

Motion picture apparatus. 2,123,624. July 12, 1938. [With C. Aalborg and O. B. French.]

Refrigerating apparatus. 2,148,412. February 21, 1939.

Receiving system. 2,151,747. March 28, 1939.

Alternating-current direct-current clock. 2,183,062. December 12, 1939.

Air conditioning system. 2,205,744. June 25, 1940.

Automobile battery charging system and flat rectifier therefor. 2,217,471. October 8, 1940.

Automotive generating system. 2,233,586. March 4, 1941.

Manufacture of copper-oxide rectifiers. 2,276,647. March 17, 1942. [With E. D. Wilson, C. C. Hein, and F. T. Hague.]

Title Index

Antenna system. 1,750,347.

Aperiodic receiver system. 1,515,186.

Apparatus for the receipt of wireless impulses. 1,456,867.

Armature-winding. 954,614.

Automatic synchronizer. 885,143.

Automobile battery charging system and flat rectifier therefor. 2,217,471.

Automotive generating system. 2,233,586.

Battery-charging system. 2,117,018.

Carbureter [sic]. 1,002,646.

Circuit making and breaking relay. 780,024.

Condenser. 1,837,017.

Connector. 1,318,728.

Constant current regulator. 792,120.

Constant frequency generator. 1,872,896.

Control device. 1,934,524.

Copper-oxide rectifier. 2,117,020.

Current-rectifying device. 1,112,265.

Cut-out. 1,229,719.

Directive antenna system. 1,689,863.

Distributor for ignition apparatus. 1,417,717.

Double-winding generator and rectifier combination. 2,117,019.

Duplex radio transmission system. 1,732,741.

Electric-arc lamp. 599,931.

Electric clock. 1,911,062.

Electric heating apparatus. 912,994.

Electric measuring instrument. 1,141,380.

Electric meter and motor. 608,842.

Electrical apparatus. 1,106,368.

Electrical ignition system. 1,352,432; 1,352,433.

Electrical measuring instrument. 627,908; 629,663; 794,395; 1,695,917.

Electrical regulator. 1,122,693; 1,146,925; 1,146,927.

Electrical system. 934,596; 1,191,158; 1,234,876; 1,235,012; 1,246,056; 1,260,648.

Electrical system for automobiles. 1,248,460.
Electrically operated device. 1,158,898.
Frequency-control device. 1,768,888.
Gear. 1,167,743.
Gear-shift mechanism. 1,363,719.
Gear-shifting mechanism. 1,296,483.
Gear-wheel. 1,167,742.
Ground-detector for electric circuits. 716,868.
Hand-grenade. 1,304,544.
Ignition mechanism. 1,248,459; 1,277,388.
Ignition system. 1,219,704; 1,338,360; 1,352,431; 1,352,434.
Impedance device for use with current-rectifiers. 1,075,404.
Inductance device. 1,635,541.
Inductor helix. 1,702,461.
Instrument for indicating the phase and frequency relations of
    alternating currents. 695,913.
Insulator. 1,730,124.
Interrupter. 1,171,596.
Manufacture of copper-oxide rectifiers. 2,276,647.
Means for measuring the energy of three-phase alternating-
    current circuits. 716,867.
Means for protecting electrical systems. 1,155,134.
Measuring instrument. 798,167.
Measuring the energy of three-phase alternating-current
    circuits. 717,496.
Mercury-vapor rectifier. 969,525.
Metering system. 1,029,743.
Modulation system. 1,799,974.
Motion-picture apparatus. 1,939,031; 2,023,065; 2,032,116;
    2,123,624.
Mounting for oil-pumps. 1,344,756.
Multiple electrode vacuum tube. 1,709,659.
Overload and reverse current relay. 1,137,840.
Overload and reverse current relay device. 933,746; 934,390;
    934,391.
Plug-connector. 1,175,343.

Polyphase plate-circuit excitation system. 1,645,291.
Prepayment electrical measuring device. 757,439.
Prepayment-meter. 1,017,082.
Pressure-gage. 1,150,016.
Priming device for internal-combustion engines. 1,271,670.
Protective apparatus for electrical circuits. 840,478.
Protective apparatus for parallel transmission-lines. 840,479.
Protective means for electrical systems. 1,155,133.
Radio communication system. 2,057,640.
Radio relay system. 1,877,815.
Radio sending system. 1,654,322.
Radio transmitting system. 1,652,516.
Radiomodulation system. 1,477,316.
Radiotelegraphy system. 1,314,789.
Receiving circuit for the elimination of static disturbances.
    1,513,223.
Receiving system. 2,151,747.
Recording measuring instrument. 1,031,041; 1,031,042.
Rectifier system. 1,112,266.
Refrigerating apparatus. 2,148,412.
Refrigerator. 1,982,375.
Refrigerator apparatus. 2,056,646.
Regulating means for systems of electrical distribution.
    807,943.
Regulator and cut-out. 1,260,647; 1,260,649.
Regulator for electrical circuits. 1,146,926.
Regulator system. 1,543,696.
Safety device for starting motors. 1,130,573.
Short-wave antenna. 1,768,666.
Side lamp for automobiles. 1,296,482.
Signaling system. 1,563,342.
Spark-advancer. 1,171,594.
Spark-advancing mechanism. 1,466,272.
Spring-abutment for measuring instruments. 798,168.
Starting and ignition machine. 1,237,172.
Starting-electrode for vapor electric devices. 1,194,143.

Starting means for vapor electric devices. 1,166,186.
Starting means for vapor-rectifying devices. 975,399.
Starting mechanism for automobiles. 1,175,342; 1,215,490;
    1,246,057; 1,385,983.
Starting mechanism for gas-engines. 1,317,269; 1,370,005.
Starting mechanism for internal-combustion engines.
    1,413,829.
Starting motor for gas-engines. 1,246,718.
Starting system for automobiles. 1,246,717; 1,274,992.
Storage-battery regulator. 1,146,924.
Switch for electric circuits. 803,212.
System for vapor electric apparatus. 931,114.
System of distribution. 1,108,886.
System of distribution for mercury-vapor rectifiers. 931,115.
System of electric-motor control. 1,024,557.
System of electrical distribution. 1,138,637; 1,159,904;
    1,224,143; 1,320,083.
System of electrical distribution and regulation. 1,112,438.
Telephone circuits and apparatus. 1,693,401.
Telephone device. 1,660,864; 1,680,409.
Telephone receiver. 1,819,499.
Television apparatus. 1,991,082.
Television system. 1,853,661.
Time switch. 2,121,585.
Transformer. 829,572; 841,076; 1,005,163.
Transformer for use with current-rectifying apparatus.
    1,123,248.
Transmission system. 1,939,042.
Tuning system of antennae. 1,502,848.
Vapor-arc rectifier. 1,264,276.
Vapor current-rectifying device. 1,234,875.
Vapor electric apparatus. 1,285,947.
Vapor electric device. 1,101,523; 1,159,900.
Vapor-rectifier. 1,204,411.
Vehicle-lighting system. 1,171,595.
Volt-ampere meter. 1,571,234.

Voltage-regulator. 923,627.
Wattmeter. 1,067,311.
Wireless antenna system. 1,640,534.
Wireless receiving cabinet. 1,655,985.
Wireless receiving set. 1,664,192.
Wireless telephone system. 1,528,047.
Wireless transmission system. 1,586,653.

HARRY P. DAVIS (1868-1931)

Controlling switch for electrically-propelled vehicles. 503,279. August 15, 1893. 64:913.

Resistance-coil. 513,457. January 23, 1894. 66:641.

Method of and means for controlling electric cars. 527,947. October 23, 1894. 69:438.

Automatic-circuit breaker. 532,537. January 15, 1895. 70:316.

Controller for electric cars. 532,538. January 15, 1895. 70:317.

Non-arcing switch. 532,594. January 15, 1895. 70:334. [With Charles F. Scott.]

Electric-arc lamp. 535,051. March 5, 1895. 70:1224.

Electric-arc lamp. 535,052. March 5, 1895. 70:1224.

Combined insulator and fuse-holder. 541,459. June 25, 1895. 71:1776. [With Charles F. Scott.]

Fuse-block. 541,473. June 25, 1895. 71:1782. [With C. F. Scott.]

Rheostat element. 548,867. October 29, 1895. 73:726.

Rheostat. 559,685. May 5, 1896. 75:790.

Electric-arc lamp. 569,817. October 20, 1896. 77:393.

Electric-arc lamp. 569,818. October 20, 1896. 77:393.

Controller for electric motors. 574,885. January 12, 1897. 78:184.

Supporting means for electric-railway supply-conductors. 580,380. April 13, 1897. 79:172.

Supporting means for electric-railway supply-conductors. 580,381. April 13, 1897. 79:172.

Controller for electric cars. 582,102. May 4, 1897. 79:830. [With Albert Schmid.]

Controller for electric motors. 582,114. May 4, 1897. 79:836.

Method of and means for controlling electric motors. 582,115. May 4, 1897. 79:837.

Controller for electric motors. 584,856. June 22, 1897. 79:1900.

Quick-break switch. 599,929. March 1, 1898. 82:1304.

Switch for electric circuits. 599,930. March 1, 1898. 82:1304. [With E. F. Harder.]

Electric-arc lamp. 599,931. March 1, 1898. 82:1305. [With F. Conrad.]

Contact device for electrically-propelled vehicles. 606,819. July 5, 1898. 84:68.

Current-collecting apparatus for electric railways. 606,826. July 5, 1898. 84:72. [With Charles A. Terry.]

Overhead construction for electric railways. 606,827. July 5, 1898. 84:72. [With Charles A. Terry.]

Electric brake. 606,917. July 5, 1898. 84:99.

Regulating-switch for electric circuits. 607,617. July 19, 1898. 84:425. [With G. Wright.]

Electric meter and motor. 608,842. August 9, 1898. 84:914. [With F. Conrad.]

Controller for electric motors. 610,124. August 30, 1898. 84:1414.

Controller for electric motors. 611,465. September 27, 1898. 84:1961.

Alternating-current-measuring instrument. 611,466. September 27, 1898. 84:1962. [With F. Conrad.]

Alternating-current voltmeter. 611,592. September 27, 1898. 84:2007. [With F. Conrad.]

Circuit-breaker. 622,885. April 11, 1899. 87:260.

Controller for electric motors. 625,151. May 16, 1899. 87:1162. [With G. Wright.]

Electrical measuring instrument. 627,908. June 27, 1899. 87:2288. [With F. Conrad.]

Fuse-block for electric circuits. 629,663. July 25, 1899. 88:673.

High-tension circuit-breaker. 629,664. July 25, 1899. 88:674. [With G. Wright.]

Controller for electric motors. 629,665. July 25, 1899. 88:674. [With G. Wright.]

Fuse-block. 644,850. March 6, 1900. 90:1862.

Switch for electric circuits. 685,507. October 29, 1901. 97:868.

Resistance-coil and support therefor. 710,143. September 30, 1902. 100:2901.

Controlling induction-motors. 725,681. April 21, 1903. 103:1698.

High-tension-circuit breaker. 758,621. May 3, 1904. 110:10.

Strain device for electric railways. 791,012. May 30, 1905. 116:1243. [With T. Varney.]

Supporting and strain device for electric railways. 791,013. May 30, 1905. 116:1243. [With T. Varney.]

Trolley-wire hanger. 791,082. May 30, 1905. 116:1272. [With T. Varney.]

Curve pull-off for overhead trolley-conductors. 791,083. May 30, 1905. 116:1272. [With T. Varney.]

Circuit-breaker. 797,048. August 15, 1905. 117:1830. [With A. B. Reynders.]

Circuit-breaker. 798,171. August 29, 1905. 117:2416.

Trolley and trolley-support. 801,225. October 10, 1905. 118:1386. [With C. Aalborg.]

Trolley for electric-railway vehicles. 801,226. October 10, 1905. 118:1387. [With C. Aalborg.]

Overhead structure for electric railways. 803,215. October 31, 1905. 118:2360. [With T. Varney.]

Suspension device for trolley-conductors. 803,216. October 31, 1905. 118:2360. [With T. Varney.]

Protective apparatus for electrical circuits. 840,478. January 8, 1907. 126:404. [With F. Conrad.]

Protective apparatus for parallel transmission-lines. 840,479. January 8, 1907. 126:404. [With F. Conrad.]

Transformer. 841,076. January 8, 1907. 126:700. [With F. Conrad.]

Strain-insulator. 861,094. July 23, 1907. 129:1507.

Indicating means for instruments. 920,927. May 11, 1909. 142:303. [With P. MacGahan.]

Trolley-clamp. 931,390. August 17, 1909. 145:647.

Trolley-clamp. 931,391. August 17, 1909. 145:647.

Trolley-hanger. 931,392. August 17, 1909. 145:647.

Trolley-conductor hanger. 931,393. August 17, 1909. 145:648.

Trolley. 932,538. August 31, 1909. 145:1067. [With T. Varney.]

Overhead-line material for electrical railways. 933,747. September 14, 1909. 146:266

Electric-line construction. 946,537. January 18, 1910. 150:578. [With T. Varney.]

Explosion circuit-breaker. 1,009,386. November 21, 1911. 172:683. [With F. W. Harris.]

Supporting structure for trolley-conductors. 1,076,630. October 21, 1913. 195:761. [With Theodore Varney.]

Circuit-interrupter. 1,123,255. January 5, 1915. 210:18. [With C. Aalborg.]

System of electrical distribution. 1,138,637. May 11, 1915. 214:358. [With F. Conrad.]

Circuit-interrupter. 1,140,961. May 25, 1915. 214:1248. [With C. Aalborg.]

System of electrical distribution. 1,159,904. November 9, 1915. 220:558. [With Frank Conrad.]

Hand-grenade. 1,303,260. May 13, 1919. 262:177.

Tube connecter. 1,768,669. July 1, 1930.

Title Index

Alternating-current-measuring instrument. 611,466.
Alternating-current voltmeter. 611,592.

Automatic-circuit breaker. 532,537.
Circuit-breaker. 622,885; 797,048; 798,171.
Circuit-interrupter. 1,123,255; 1,140,961.
Combined insulator and fuse-holder. 541,459.
Contact device for electrically-propelled vehicles. 606,819.
Controller for electric cars. 532,538; 582,102.
Controller for electric motors. 574,885; 582,114; 584,856;
    610;124; 611,465; 625,151; 629,665.
Controlling induction-motors. 725,681.
Controlling switch for electrically-propelled vehicles. 503,279.
Current-collecting apparatus for electric railways. 606,826.
Curve pull-off for overhead trolley-conductors. 791,083.
Electric-arc lamp. 535,051; 535,052, 569,817; 569,818;
    599,931.
Electric brake. 606,917.
Electric-line construction. 946,537.
Electric meter and motor. 608,842.
Electrical measuring instrument. 627,908.
Explosion circuit-breaker. 1,009,386.
Fuse-block. 541,473; 644,850.
Fuse-block for electric circuits. 629,663.
Hand-grenade. 1,303,260.
High-tension circuit-breaker. 629,664; 758,621.
Indicating means for instruments. 920,927.
Method of and means for controlling electric cars. 527,947.
Method of and means for controlling electric motors. 582,115.
Non-arcing switch. 532,594.
Overhead construction for electric railways. 606,827.
Overhead-line material for electrical railways. 933,747.
Overhead structure for electric railways. 803,215.
Protective apparatus for electrical circuits. 840,478.
Protective apparatus for parallel transmission-lines. 840,479.
Quick-break switch. 599,929.
Regulating-switch for electric circuits. 607,617.
Resistance-coil. 513,457.
Resistance-coil and support therefor. 710,143.

Rheostat. 559,685.
Rheostat element. 548,867.
Strain device for electric railways. 791,012.
Strain-insulator. 861,094.
Supporting and strain device for electric railways. 791,013.
Supporting means for electric-railway supply-conductors.
    580,380; 580,381.
Supporting structure for trolley-conductors. 1,076,630.
Suspension device for trolley-conductors. 803,216.
Switch for electric circuits. 599,930; 685,507.
System of electrical distribution. 1,138,637; 1,159,904.
Transformer. 841,076.
Trolley. 932,538.
Trolley and trolley-support. 801,225.
Trolley-clamp. 931,390; 931,391.
Trolley-conductor hanger. 931,393.
Trolley for electric-railway vehicles. 801,226.
Trolley-hanger. 931,392.
Trolley-wire hanger. 791,082.
Tube connecter. 1,768,669.

LEE de FOREST (1873-1961)

[Note: Patents assigned to any of the various de Forest companies but not in de Forest's name are not listed.]

Apparatus for communicating signals through space. 716,000. December 16, 1902. 101:2412. [With E. H. Smythe.]

Wireless telegraphy. 716,203. December 16, 1902. 101:2501. [With E. H. Smythe.]

Communicating signals through space. 716,334. December 16, 1902. 101:2548. [With E. H. Smythe.]

Space telegraphy. 720,568. February 17, 1903. 102:1308.

Space telegraphy. 730,246. June 9, 1903. 104:1412.

Wireless telegraphy. 730,247. June 9, 1903. 104:1412.

Wireless signaling. 730,819. June 9, 1903. 104:1629.

Wireless signaling device. 748,597. January 5, 1904. 108:19.

Wireless signaling apparatus. 749,131. January 5, 1904. 108:269.

Wireless signaling apparatus. 749,178. January 12, 1904. 108:314.

Wireless-telegraph receiver. 749,371. January 12, 1904. 108:403.

Wireless telegraphy. 749,372. January 12, 1904. 108:404.

Wireless signaling device. 749,434. January 12, 1904. 108:429.

Generating set for wireless telegraphy. 749,435. January 12, 1904. 108:429.

Wireless-telegraph range finder. 749,436. January 12, 1904. 108:430.

Controlling spark production. 750,180. January 19, 1904. 108:758.

Device for clearing ice from antennae. 750,181. January 19, 1904. 108:758.

Wireless telegraphy. 758,517. April 26, 1904. 109:2389.

Wireless signaling apparatus. 759,216. May 3, 1904. 110:291.

Receiver for space signaling. 770,228. September 13, 1904. 112:478.

Wireless signaling apparatus. 770,229. September 13, 1904. 112:478.

Wireless signaling apparatus. 771,818. October 11, 1904. 112:1226.

Wireless signaling apparatus. 771,819. October 11, 1904. 112:1227.

Protecting device for high-frequency apparatus. 771,820. October 11, 1904. 112:1227.

Magnetic decoder. 772,878. October 18, 1904. 112:1718.

Duplex wireless telegraphy. 772,879. October 18, 1904. 112:1719.

Wireless-telegraph system. 806,966. December 12, 1905. 119:1689.

Wireless-telegraph system. 822,936. June 12, 1906. 122:2080.

Static valve for wireless-telegraph systems. 823,402. June 12, 1906. 122:2289.

Wireless-telegraph system. 824,003. June 19, 1906. 122:2606.

Oscillation-responsive device. 824,637. June 26, 1906. 122:2929.

Oscillation-responsive device. 824,638. June 26, 1906. 122:2930.

Wireless-telegraph system. 827,523. July 31, 1906. 123:1542.

Wireless-telegraph system. 827,524. July 31, 1906. 123:1543.

Aerophore. 833,034. October 9, 1906. 124:1739.

Aerophone. 836,015. November 13, 1906. 125:587.

Oscillation-responsive device. 836,070. November 13, 1906. 125:613.

Oscillation-responsive device. 836,071. November 13, 1906. 125:613.

Aerophone. 836,072. November 13, 1906. 125:614.

Wireless telegraphy. 837,901. December 4, 1906. 125:1658.

Wireless telegraphy. 841,386. January 15, 1907. 126:906.

Device for amplifying feeble electrical currents. 841,387. January 15, 1907. 126:908.

Space telegraphy. 850,917. April 23, 1907. 127:2834.

Wireless-telegraph receiving system. 852,381. April 30, 1907. 127:3599.

Oscillation responsive device. 867,876. October 8, 1907. 130:1638.

Detecting oscillations. 867,877. October 8, 1907. 130:1639.

Oscillation-detector. 867,878. October 8, 1907. 130:1639.

Cautery. 874,178. December 17, 1907. 131:1849.

Wireless-telegraph transmitting system. 876,165. January 7, 1908. 132:158.

Magnetic detector. 877,069. January 21, 1908. 132:531.

Space telegraphy. 879,532. February 18, 1908. 132:1458.

Electrode for electrolytic or liquid oscillation-detectors for wireless telegraphy. 894,317. July 28, 1908. 135:717.

Aerophore. 894,318. July 28, 1908. 135:717.

Wireless signaling apparatus. 894,378. July 28, 1908. 135:736.

Space telegraphy. 913,718. March 2, 1909. 140:16.

Wireless telegraphy. 926,933. July 6, 1909. 144:76.

Wireless-telegraph tuning device. 926,934. July 6, 1909. 144:77.

Wireless-telegraph transmitter. 926,935. July 6, 1909. 144:77.

Space telegraphy. 926,936. July 6, 1909. 144:77.

Space telephony. 926,937. July 6, 1909. 144:78.

Space telegraphy. 943,969. December 21, 1909. 149:720.

Transmitting apparatus. 966,539. August 9, 1910. 157:260.

Aerophone. 973,644. October 25, 1910. 159:815.

Oscillation-responsive device. 979,275. December 20, 1910. 161:696.

Space telegraphy. 979,276. December 20, 1910. 161:696.

High-frequency electrical-oscillation generator. 979,277. December 20, 1910. 161:697.

System for amplifying feeble electric currents. 995,126. June 13, 1911. 167:391.

Space telegraphy. 995,339. June 13, 1911. 167:461.

Space telephony. 1,006,635. October 24, 1911. 171:818.

Space telephony. 1,006,636. October 24, 1911. 171:818.

Transmission of music by electromagnetic waves. 1,025,908. May 7, 1912. 178:275.

Score-card. 1,026,433. May 14, 1912. 178:491.

System of duplex wireless transmission. 1,042,205. October 22, 1912. 183:955.

Wireless telegraphy. 1,101,533. June 30, 1914. 203:1273.

Signaling system. 1,123,118. December 29, 1914. 209:1626.

Secrecy system for wireless communication. 1,123,119. December 29, 1914. 209:1627.

Arc mechanism for systems of space communications. 1,123,120. December 29, 1914. 209:1627.

Wireless-telephone transmitting system. 1,125,496. January 19, 1915. 210:888.

Receiving system for electromagnetic radiations. 1,134,593. April 6, 1915. 213:186.

Means for increasing the strength of electric currents. 1,134,594. April 6, 1915. 213:187.

Wireless receiving system. 1,170,881. February 8, 1916. 223:428.

Automatic switching device for telephone systems. 1,170,882. February 8, 1916. 223:428.

Spark-gap for radiotone wireless-telegraph systems. 1,171,598. February 15, 1916. 223:722.

Apparatus for and method of recording fluctuating currents. 1,177,848. April 4, 1916. 225:94.

Range-teller. 1,183,802. May 16, 1916. 226:1030.

Wireless telephone system. 1,183,803. May 16, 1916. 226:1031.

Quench-spark discharger. 1,190,869. July 11, 1916. 228:631.

Oscillating-current generator. 1,201,270. October 17, 1916. 231:624.

Oscillating audion. 1,201,271. October 17, 1916. 231:624.

Telegraph and telephone receiving system. 1,201,272. October 17, 1916. 231:625.

Oscillation-generator. 1,201,273. October 17, 1916. 231:625.

Wireless telegraphy. 1,214,283. January 30, 1917. 234:1479.

Wireless-telegraph signaling system. 1,221,033. April 3, 1917. 237:11.

Oscillating-current generator. 1,221,034. April 3, 1917. 237:11.

Apparatus for use in wire or radio communications. 1,221,035. April 3, 1917. 237:11.

Metallic audion. 1,230,874. June 26, 1917. 239:959.

Apparatus for use in radiocommunication. 1,299,356. April 1, 1919. 261:168.

Means for transforming mechanical vibrations into electrical vibrations. 1,309,753. July 15, 1919. 264:388.

Oscillation-generator. 1,311,264. July 29, 1919. 264:729.

Method of and means for reproducing and amplifying weak pulsating currents. 1,314,250. August 26, 1919. 265:538.

Radiotelephony. 1,314,251. August 26, 1919. 265:538.

Oscillation-generator. 1,314,252. August 26, 1919. 265:538.

Apparatus for use in wire or radio communications. 1,314,253. August 26, 1919. 265:538.

Oscillating-current generator. 1,329,758. February 3, 1920. 271:77.

Apparatus for amplifying pulsating electric currents. 1,348,157. August 3, 1920. 277:5.

Radio-telephone system. 1,348,213. August 3, 1920. 277:16.

Wireless telephone system. Reissue 14,959. October 19, 1920. 279:497.

Apparatus for use in telegraphy or telephony. 1,365,157. January 11, 1921. 282:258.

Endless-film arrangement. 1,365,237. January 11, 1921. 282:273.

Means for amplifying currents. 1,375,447. April 19, 1921. 285:503.

Audion-circuit. 1,377,405. May 10, 1921. 286:253.

Selective audion amplifier. 1,397,575. November 22, 1921.

Radiosignaling system. 1,417,662. May 30, 1922.

Subterranean signaling system. 1,424,805. August 8, 1922.

Oscillion. 1,437,498. December 5, 1922.

Sound-controlled means for producing light variations. 1,442,426. January 16, 1923.

Endless sound record and mechanism therefor. 1,442,682. January 16, 1923.

Means for transforming mechanical vibrations into electrical vibrations. Reissue 15,540. February 13, 1923.

Means for recording and reproducing sound. 1,446,246. February 20, 1923.

Light-controlling means. 1,446,247. February 20, 1923.

Telephone device. 1,452,827. April 24, 1923.

Method of and means for controlling electric currents by and in accordance with light variation. 1,466,701. September 4, 1923.

Radio receiving system. 1,478,029. December 18, 1923.

Means for recording and reproducing sound. 1,482,119. January 29, 1924.

Sound producer. 1,486,866. March 18, 1924.

Recording sound. 1,489,314. April 8, 1924.

Radio signaling system. 1,507,016. September 2, 1924.

Wireless telegraph and telephone system. 1,507,017. September 2, 1924.

Communication system for railway trains. 1,515,152. November 11, 1924.

Thermophone. 1,526,778. February 17, 1925.

Electrical means for producing musical notes. 1,543,990. June 30, 1925.

Telephone device. 1,552,914. September 8, 1925.

Sound-reproducing mechanism. 1,554,561. September 22, 1925.

Loud-speaking device. 1,554,794. September 22, 1925.

Radio signaling system. 1,554,795. September 22, 1925.

Sound-reproducing device. 1,560,502. November 3, 1925.

Indicating device for fluid tanks. 1,561,596. November 17, 1925.

Loud speaker. Reissue 69,443. February 16, 1926.

Railway signaling system. 1,610,692. December 14, 1926. [Charles V. Logwood, assignor.]

Recording sound. 1,618,641. February 22, 1927.

Slot cleaner for motion-picture machines. 1,629,152. May 17, 1927.

Electrical sound-reproducing apparatus. 1,641,664. September 6, 1927.

Telephone device. 1,642,363. September 13, 1927.

Talking-moving-picture equipment. 1,653,155. December 20, 1927.

Film-protecting arrangement. 1,659,909. February 21, 1928.

Slot cleaner for phonofilm attachment for motion-picture machines. 1,659,910. February 21, 1928.

Radio signaling system. 1,680,207. August 7, 1928.

Sound recording and reproducing apparatus. 1,683,451. September 4, 1928.

Radio transmitting system. 1,687,364. October 9, 1928.

Sound-recording attachment for motion-picture cameras. 1,693,071. November 27, 1928.

Shielding sound detector and amplifier apparatus. 1,693,072. November 27, 1928.

Talking-moving-picture machine. 1,695,414. December 18, 1928.

Talking-moving-picture record. 1,695,415. December 18, 1928.

Acoustic apparatus. 1,701,911. February 12, 1929.

Motion-picture screen. 1,710,922. April 30, 1929.

Producing talking-motion-picture films and apparatus used therefor. 1,716,033. June 4, 1929.

Loud-speaker motor. 1,718,337. June 25, 1929.

Radio receiving apparatus. 1,720,544. July 9, 1929.

Photo-electric cell. 1,722,280. July 30, 1929.

Diffraction microphone. 1,726,289. August 27, 1929.

Sound-reproducing device. 1,736,035. November 19, 1929.

Sound actuated and producing device. 1,738,988. December 10, 1929.

Wireless telegraph and telephone system. 1,740,577. December 24, 1929.

Sound and picture recording camera. 1,761,619. June 3, 1930.

Producing talking-motion-picture films. 1,764,938. June 17, 1930.

Sound-reproducing device. 1,766,612. June 24, 1930.

Binaural recording and reproducing sound. 1,769,907. July 1, 1930.

Recording and reproducing sound. 1,769,908. July 1, 1930.

Switch mechanism for talking-motion-picture-exciting lamps. 1,769,909. July 1, 1930.

Binaural recording and reproducing sound. 1,777,037. September 30, 1930.

Sound-picture photography. 1,777,828. October 7, 1930.

Loud-speaker. 1,785,377. December 16, 1930. [With R. Halpenny.]

Sound reproducer. 1,795,936. March 10, 1931.

Automatic photographic sound reproducing mechanism. 1,802,595. April 28, 1931.

Silent drive mechanism for talking motion picture machines. 1,806,744. May 26, 1931.

Sound producing device. 1,806,745. May 26, 1931.

Luminous discharge device. 1,806,746. May 26, 1931.

Talking motion pictures and obliterating stipulated portion or portions therefor. Reissue 18,108. June 23, 1931.

Sound-chamber and set-frame therefor. 1,812,687. June 30, 1931.

Sound reproducer. 1,827,283. October 13, 1931.

Microphone. 1,834,051. December 1, 1931.

Talking motion picture apparatus. 1,843,972. February 9, 1932.

Sound reproducing device. 1,853,850. April 12, 1932.

Sound-on-film phonograph. 1,859,435. May 24, 1932.

Sound reproducing device. 1,866,090. July 5, 1932.

Gaseous discharge device. 1,873,558. August 23, 1932.

Talking motion picture attachment. 1,885,900. November 1, 1932.

Securing synchronization in talking motion picture photography. 1,888,910. November 22, 1932.

Photographic sound reproducing apparatus. 1,894,024. January 10, 1933.

Luminous discharge device. 1,897,363. February 14, 1933.

Soundproofing picture recording camera. 1,929,626. October 10, 1933.

Gaseous discharge device. 1,944,929. January 30, 1934.

Apparatus for reproducing sound-on-film. 1,992,201. February 26, 1935.

Television receiving and projecting. 2,003,680. June 4, 1935.

Television receiving method and apparatus. 2,026,872. January 7, 1936.

Apparatus for receiving and projecting televised images in synchronism with sound. 2,045,570. June 30, 1936.

Television sign. 2,049,763. August 4, 1936.

Television apparatus. 2,052,133. August 25, 1936.

Apparatus for reproducing sound-on-film. 2,064,593. December 15, 1936.

Television system and method. 2,122,456. July 5, 1938.

High frequency oscillating circuit. 2,126,541. August 9, 1938.

Radial scanning television system. 2,163,749. June 27, 1939.

Television radial scanning system employing cathode beam. 2,241,809. May 13, 1941. [Assigned to R. C. Gilman, Waterbury, Conn.]

Method of and apparatus for determining the ground speed and/or course of aircraft. 2,391,554. December 25, 1945.

Altitude determination. 2,410,868. November 12, 1946.

Method of and apparatus for determining absolute altitude. 2,421,248. May 27, 1947.

Color television system. 2,452,293. October 26, 1948.

Method of and apparatus for bunching electrons. 2,457,980. January 4, 1949.

Cathode beam tube. 2,457,981. January 4, 1949.

Frequency modulating device. 2,462,367. February 22, 1949.

High-voltage generator. 2,489,082. November 22, 1949.

Electronic light amplifier. 2,594,740. April 29, 1952. [With W. A. Rhodes.]

Apparatus for color television. 2,617,875. November 11, 1952.

Transistor. 2,735,049. February 14, 1956.

Method and apparatus for recording and reproducing television pictures. 2,743,318. April 24, 1956.

Automatic dialing device for dial telephones. 2,813,931. November 19, 1957.

Title Index

Acoustic apparatus. 1,701,911.
Aerophone. 836,015; 836,072; 973,644.
Aerophore. 833,034; 894,318.
Altitude determination. 2,410,868.
Apparatus for amplifying pulsating electric currents.
    1,348,157.
Apparatus for and method of recording fluctuating currents.
    1,177,848.
Apparatus for color television. 2,617,875.
Apparatus for communicating signals through space. 716,000.
Apparatus for receiving and projecting televised images in
    synchronism with sound. 2,045,570.
Apparatus for reproducing sound-on-film. 1,992,201;
    2,064,593.
Apparatus for use in radiocommunication. 1,299,356.
Apparatus for use in telegraphy or telephony. 1,365,157.
Apparatus for use in wire or radio communications.
    1,221,035; 1,314,253.

Arc mechanism for systems of space communications. 1,123,120.

Audion. *See* 879,532.

Audion-circuit. 1,377,405.

Automatic dialing device for dial telephones. 2,813,931.

Automatic photographic sound reproducing mechanism. 1,802,595.

Automatic switching device for telephone systems. 1,170,882.

Binaural recording and reproducing sound. 1,769,907; 1,777,037.

Cathode beam tube. 2,457,981.

Cautery. 874,178.

Color television system. 2,452,293.

Communicating signals through space. 716,334..

Communication system for railway trains. 1,515,152.

Controlling spark production. 750,180.

Detecting oscillations. 867,877.

Device for amplifying feeble electrical currents. 841,387.

Device for clearing ice from antennae. 750,181.

Diffraction microphone. 1,726,289.

Duplex wireless telegraphy. 772,879.

Electrical means for producing musical notes. 1,543,990.

Electrical sound-reproducing apparatus. 1,641,664.

Electrode for electrolytic or liquid oscillation-detectors for wireless telegraphy. 894,317.

Electronic light amplifier. 2,594,740.

Endless-film arrangement. 1,365,237.

Endless sound record and mechanism therefor. 1,442,682.

Film-protecting arrangement. 1,659,909.

Frequency modulating device. 2,462,367.

Gaseous discharge device. 1,873,558; 1,944,929.

Generating set for wireless telegraphy. 749,435.

Grid leak. *See* 1,377,405.

High-frequency electrical-oscillation generator. 979,277.

High frequency oscillating circuit. 2,126,541.

High-voltage generator. 2,489,082.

Indicating device for fluid tanks. 1,561,596.
Light-controlling means. 1,446,247.
Loud speaker. Reissue 69,443. February 16, 1926.
Loud-speaker. 1,785,377.
Loud-speaker motor. 1,718,337.
Loud-speaking device. 1,554,794.
Luminous discharge device. 1,806,746; 1,897,363.
Magnetic decoder. 772,878.
Magnetic detector. 877,069.
Means for amplifying currents. 1,375,447.
Means for increasing the strength of electric currents.
    1,134,594.
Means for recording and reproducing sound. 1,446,246;
    1,482,119.
Means for transforming mechanical vibrations into electrical
    vibrations. 1,309,753.
Means for transforming mechanical vibrations into electrical
    vibrations. Reissue 15,540. February 13, 1923.
Metallic audion. 1,230,874.
Method and apparatus for recording and reproducing television
    pictures. 2,743,318.
Method of and apparatus for bunching electrons. 2,457,980.
Method of and apparatus for determining absolute altitude.
    2,421,248.
Method of and apparatus for determining the ground speed
    and/or course of aircraft. 2,391,554.
Method of and means for controlling electric currents by and
    in accordance with light variation. 1,466,701.
Method of and means for reproducing and amplifying weak
    pulsating currents. 1,314,250.
Microphone. 1,834,051.
Motion-picture screen. 1,710,922.
Oscillating audion. 1,201,271.
Oscillating-current generator. 1,201,270; 1,221,034;
    1,329,758.
Oscillation-detector. 867,878.

Oscillation-generator. 1,201,273; 1,311,264; 1,314,252.
Oscillation-responsive device. 824,637; 824,638; 836,070; 836,071; 867,876; 979,275.
Oscillion. 1,437,498.
Photo-electric cell. 1,722,280.
Photographic sound reproducing apparatus. 1,894,024.
Producing talking-motion-picture films. 1,764,938.
Producing talking-motion-picture films and apparatus used therefor. 1,716,033.
Protecting device for high-frequency apparatus. 771,820.
Quench-spark discharger. 1,190,869.
Radial scanning television system. 2,163,749.
Radio receiving apparatus. 1,720,544.
Radio receiving system. 1,478,029.
Radiosignaling system. 1,417,662.
Radio signaling system. 1,507,016; 1,554,795; 1,680,207.
Radio-telephone system. 1,348,213.
Radiotelephony. 1,314,251.
Radio transmitting system. 1,687,364.
Railway signaling system. 1,610,692.
Range-teller. 1,183,802.
Receiver for space signaling. 770,228.
Receiving system for electromagnetic radiations. 1,134,593.
Recording and reproducing sound. 1,769,908.
Recording sound. 1,489,314; 1,618,641.
Score-card. 1,026,433.
Secrecy system for wireless communication. 1,123,119.
Securing synchronization in talking motion picture photography. 1,888,910.
Selective audion amplifier. 1,397,575.
Shielding sound detector and amplifier apparatus. 1,693,072.
Signaling system. 1,123,118.
Silent drive mechanism for talking motion picture machines. 1,806,744.
Slot cleaner for motion-picture machines. 1,629,152.

Slot cleaner for phonofilm attachment for motion-picture
machines. 1,659,910.
Sound actuated and producing device. 1,738,988.
Sound and picture recording camera. 1,761,619.
Sound-chamber and set-frame therefor. 1,812,687.
Sound-controlled means for producing light variations.
1,442,426.
Sound-on-film phonograph. 1,859,435.
Sound-picture photography. 1,777,828.
Sound producer. 1,486,866.
Sound producing device. 1,806,745.
Sound recording and reproducing apparatus. 1,683,451.
Sound-recording attachment for motion-picture cameras.
1,693,071.
Sound reproducer. 1,795,936; 1,827,283.
Sound-reproducing device. 1,560,502; 1,736,035; 1,766,612;
1,853,850; 1,866,090.
Sound-reproducing mechanism. 1,554,561.
Soundproofing picture recording camera. 1,929,626.
Space telegraphy. 720,568; 730,246; 850,917; 879,532;
913,718; 926,936; 943,969; 979,276; 995,339.
Space telephony. 926,937; 1,006,635; 1,006,636.
Spark-gap for radiotone wireless-telegraph systems.
1,171,598.
Static valve for wireless-telegraph systems. 823,402.
Subterranean signaling system. 1,424,805.
Switch mechanism for talking-motion-picture-exciting lamps.
1,769,909.
System for amplifying feeble electric currents. 995,126.
System of duplex wireless transmission. 1,042,205.
Talking motion picture apparatus. 1,843,972.
Talking motion picture attachment. 1,885,900.
Talking motion pictures and obliterating stipulated portion or
portions therefor. Reissue 18,108. June 23, 1931.
Talking-moving-picture equipment. 1,653,155.
Talking-moving-picture machine. 1,695,414.

Talking-moving-picture record. 1,695,415.
Telegraph and telephone receiving system. 1,201,272.
Telephone device. 1,452,827; 1,552,914; 1,642,363.
Television apparatus. 2,052,133.
Television radial scanning system employing cathode beam.
    2,241,809.
Television receiving and projecting. 2,003,680.
Television receiving method and apparatus. 2,026,872.
Television sign. 2,049,763.
Television system and method. 2,122,456.
Thermophone. 1,526,778.
Transistor. 2,735,049.
Transmission of music by electromagnetic waves. 1,025,908.
Transmitting apparatus. 966,539.
Wireless receiving system. 1,170,881.
Wireless signaling. 730,819.
Wireless signaling apparatus. 749,131; 749,178; 759,216;
    770,229; 771,818; 771,819; 894,378.
Wireless signaling device. 748,597; 749,434.
Wireless telegraph and telephone system. 1,507,017;
    1,740,577.
Wireless-telegraph range finder. 749,436.
Wireless-telegraph receiver. 749,371.
Wireless-telegraph receiving system. 852,381.
Wireless-telegraph signaling system. 1,221,033.
Wireless-telegraph system. 806,966; 822,936; 824,003;
    827,523; 827,524.
Wireless-telegraph transmitter. 926,935.
Wireless-telegraph transmitting system. 876,165.
Wireless-telegraph tuning device. 926,934.
Wireless telegraphy. 716,203; 730,247; 749,372; 758,517;
    837,901; 841,386; 926,933; 1,101,533; 1,214,283.
Wireless telephone system. 1,183,803.
Wireless telephone system. Reissue 14,959. October 19, 1920.
Wireless-telephone transmitting system. 1,125,496.

AMOS DOLBEAR (1837-1910)

Telephone. 199,041. January 18, 1878. 13:67.

Book-support. 204,427. June 4, 1878. 13:1014.

Combined speaking-telephone and Morse sounder. 220,205. September 30, 1879. 16:623.

Combined telephone and electro-magnet. 226,906. April 27, 1880. 17:730.

Apparatus for transmitting sound by electricity. 239,742. April 5, 1891. 19:822.

Transmitting sound by electricity. 240,578. April 26, 1891. 19:1021.

Telephone. 257,133. April 25, 1882. 21:1269. [With A. H. Hieatzman.]

Telephone. 288,215. November 13, 1883. 25:608.

Telephone system. 325,659. September 8, 1885. 32:1131.

Increasing the efficiency of telephones. 325,660. September 8, 1885. 32:1132.

Mode of electric communication. 350,299. October 5, 1886. 37:55.

Telephone-receiver. 355,149. December 28, 1886. 37:1432.

Electric cable. 373,394. November 15, 1887. 41:800. [With F. M. Holmes.]

Title Index

WILLIAM DUBILIER (1888-1969)

[Note: Patents assigned to Dubilier Condenser and Radio Corporation but not in Dubilier's name are not listed.]

High-frequency apparatus. 1,004,152. September 26, 1911. 170:775.

High-frequency apparatus. 1,023,135. April 16, 1912. 177:537.

Electric heater. 1,079,225. November 18, 1913. 196:747.

Electrode device for high-frequency apparatus. 1,121,077. December 15, 1914. 209:842.

Wireless apparatus and method therefor. 1,279,850. September 24, 1918. 254:765.

Protective unit. 1,281,309. October 15, 1918. 255:386.

Electrical-discharge-producing device. 1,307,854. June 24, 1919. 263:583. [With P. Dubilier.]

Series condenser. 1,327,593. January 6, 1920. 270:133.

Condenser. 1,334,139. March 16, 1920. 272:484.

Condenser and adjusting same. 1,334,140. March 16, 1920. 272:484.

Insulation-testing device. 1,334,141. March 16, 1920.
272:484.

Condenser-plate construction. 1,334,142. March 16, 1920.
272:485.

Condenser and making same. 1,345,754. July 6, 1920.
276:84.

Self-protecting condenser. 1,350,010. August 17, 1920.
277:491.

Radiosignaling apparatus. 1,382,177. June 21, 1921. 287:462.
[With P. Dubilier.]

Electrical condenser. 1,391,672. September 27, 1921.
290:653.

Antenna-shortening device. 1,391,673. September 27, 1921.
290:653.

Variable condenser. 1,396,030. November 8, 1921.

Variable condenser. 1,429,227. September 19, 1922.

Electrical condenser. 1,455,781. May 22, 1923.

Razor holder. 1,475,940. December 4, 1923. [With W. S.
Mountford.]

Multifrequency generator. 1,477,271. December 11, 1923.
[With F. Lowenstein.]

Electrical apparatus. 1,485,462. March 4, 1924. [With F.
Lowenstein.]

Terminal connection for condensers. 1,480,604. January 15, 1924.

Electrical condenser. 1,497,095. June 10, 1924.

Electrical condenser. 1,526,664. February 17, 1925.

Electrical condenser. 1,537,660. May 12, 1925.

Electrical condenser for ignition circuits. 1,541,630. June 9, 1925.

Condenser and clamp therefor. 1,543,326. June 23, 1925.

Insulating structure for high-potential condensers. 1,565,799. December 15, 1925.

Electrical condenser. 1,571,512. February 2, 1926.

Electrical condenser. 1,575,044. March 2, 1926.

Electrical condenser. 1,575,045. March 2, 1926.

Condenser structure. 1,587,942. June 8, 1926.

Electrical condenser. Design 70,547. July 13, 1926.

Electrical condenser. Design 70,548. July 13, 1926.

Telephone receiver. 1,602,814. October 12, 1926.

Condenser construction. 1,603,939. October 19, 1926.

Method and apparatus for interrupting electrical circuits. 1,623,531. April 5, 1927.

Electrical condenser. 1,627,493. May 3, 1927.

Electrical structure. 1,628,627. May 10, 1927.

Mousetrap. 1,630,241. May 24, 1927. [With W. S. Mountford.]

Condenser. 1,639,597. August 16, 1927.

High-potential condenser. 1,639,650. August 23, 1927.

Variable condenser. 1,646,236. October 18, 1927.

Insulating structure for high-potential condenser terminals and the like. 1,650,983. November 29, 1927.

Carrier-wave coupler. 1,657,248. January 24, 1928.

Electrical condenser. 1,671,519. May 29, 1928.

Grid-leak resistance. 1,683,067. September 4, 1928.

Electrical condenser. 1,688,960. October 23, 1928.

Electrical condenser. 1,688,961. October 23, 1928.

Electric flasher device. 1,692,292. November 20, 1928.

Electrical resistance. 1,694,167. December 4, 1928.

Tube reviver. 1,698,625. January 8, 1929.

Variable condenser. 1,705,242. March 12, 1929.

Radio appliance. 1,705,559. March 19, 1929.

Electrical condenser. 1,710,412. April 23, 1929.

Electrical condenser. 1,713,867. May 21, 1929.

Variable condenser. 1,714,662. May 28, 1929.

Connecting device for radio receiving systems. 1,717,701.
June 18, 1929.

Condenser. 1,718,278. June 25, 1929.

Condenser. 1,722,325. July 30, 1929.

Variable condenser. 1,722,326. July 30, 1929.

Controlling device. 1,728,045. September 10, 1929.

Spark plug. 1,729,248. September 24, 1929.

Electrostatic condenser. 1,731,652. October 15, 1929.

Electrical condenser. 1,731,653. October 15, 1929.

Variable condenser. 1,735,532. November 12, 1929.

Condenser. 1,737,752. December 3, 1929.

Adjustable vacuum condenser. 1,738,175. December 3, 1929.

Variable condenser. 1,740,159. December 17, 1929.

Support for resistances. 1,740,160. December 17, 1929.

Electrical condenser. 1,742,759. January 7, 1930.

Grid leak and condenser. 1,744,301. January 21, 1930.

High-potential condenser. 1,744,454. January 21, 1930.

Variable condenser. 1,750,393. March 11, 1930.

Electrical condenser. 1,754,268. April 15, 1930.

Loud-speaker. 1,755,636. April 22, 1930.

Variable condenser. 1,756,512. April 29, 1930.

Electrical condenser. 1,757,657. May 6, 1930.

Electric sadiron. 1,757,658. May 6, 1930.

Electrical structure. 1,759,230. May 20, 1930.

Variable condenser. 1,763,554. June 10, 1930.

Condenser. 1,768,439. June 24, 1930.

Condenser kit. 1,768,440. June 24, 1930.

Electrical condenser. 1,768,441. June 24, 1930.

Electrical condenser. 1,768,442. June 24, 1930.

Lamp socket. 1,779,804. October 28, 1930.

Process and apparatus for making electric condensers. 1,785,479. December 16, 1930.

Indicating device for high frequency currents. 1,802,077. April 21, 1931.

Electrical condenser. 1,816,640. July 28, 1931.

Electrical condenser. 1,816,641. July 28, 1931.

Electrical condenser. 1,821,055. September 1, 1931.

Electrical condenser. 1,824,805. September 29, 1931.

Electrical condenser. 1,824,806. September 29, 1931.

Electrical condenser. 1,829,891. November 3, 1931.

Dimming lamps. 1,830,531. November 3, 1931.

Electrical condenser. 1,833,392. November 24, 1931.

Electrical condenser. 1,836,707. December 15, 1931.

Circuit breaker. 1,838,664. December 29, 1931.

Variable condenser. 1,841,095. January 12, 1932.

Power factor condenser. 1,842,374. January 26, 1932.

Condenser. 1,848,215. March 8, 1932.

Variometer. 1,861,052. May 31, 1932.

Electrical condenser. 1,862,302. June 7, 1932.

Electrical condenser. 1,870,797. August 9, 1932.

Electrical condenser unit. 1,870,948. August 9, 1932.

Rolled condenser. 1,870,949. August 9, 1932.

Electrical condenser. 1,870,950. August 9, 1932.

Condenser. 1,870,961. August 9, 1932. [With A. Nyman.]

Adjustable condenser. 1,871,048. August 9, 1932.

Electrical structure. 1,874,936. August 30, 1932.

Flasher device. 1,898,174. February 21, 1933.

Making electrical condensers. 1,926,842. September 12, 1933.

High frequency small capacity condenser. 1,937,010. November 28, 1933.

Wired radio communication system. 1,944,226. January 23, 1934.

Power tractor condenser. 1,945,108. January 30, 1934.

Electromagnetic operating mechanism. 2,023,355. December 3, 1935.

High tension generator. 2,038,553. April 28, 1936.

Electrical condenser. 2,043,532. June 9, 1936.

High tension generator. 2,047,463. July 14, 1936.

Electric condenser. 2,075,891. April 6, 1937.

Dielectric composition. 2,088,693. August 3, 1937.

Condenser. 2,127,352. August 16, 1938.

Ceramic dielectric material and making the same. 2,128,289. August 30, 1938. [With J. Oppenheimer.]

Electrical condenser. 2,128,990. September 6, 1938.

Collapsible rod. 2,130,993. September 20, 1938.

Electrical condenser. 2,133,086. October 11, 1938.

Making electrical condensers. 2,143,369. January 10, 1939.

Track system for toy trains. 2,196,257. April 9, 1940.

Collapsible table. 2,198,661. April 30, 1940.

System for controlling knitting. 2,199,336. May 7, 1940.

Fastening device, particularly rivets. 2,238,463. April 15, 1941.

Electrolytic condenser. 2,243,814. May 27, 1941.

Hearing aid amplifier. 2,257,840. October 7, 1941.

Insect screen. 2,278,538. April 7, 1942.

Electric switch. 2,284,644. June 2, 1942.

Thermostatic switch. 2,288,517. June 30, 1942.

Magnetic lock. 2,288,688. July 7, 1942.

Purse and like container. 2,288,996. July 7, 1942.

Dropper. 2,321,369. June 8, 1943.

Hearing aid system. 2,321,370. June 8, 1943.

Snap switch. 2,341,858. February 15, 1944.

Screen or webbing material. 2,355,635. August 15, 1944.

Terminal construction. 2,374,084. April 17, 1945.

Electrical capacitor. 2,398,417. April 16, 1946.

Container and terminal for electrical devices. 2,436,857. March 2, 1948.

Thermoplastic belt. 2,445,889. July 27, 1948. [With I. Rossi.]

High-voltage terminal. 2,450,273. September 28, 1948.

Device for electrically treating liquids. 2,490,730. December 6, 1949.

Electrical liquid treating device. 2,532,016. November 28, 1950.

Flexible track system for toy trains. 2,565,359. August 21, 1951.

Hearing aid. 2,566,761. September 4, 1951.

Bottle cap. 2,573,111. October 30, 1951. [With I. Rossi.]

Playing card container. 2,577,007. December 4, 1951.

Capacitor construction. 2,668,935. February 9, 1954.

Means for manufacturing metallized electrical capacitors. 2,671,157. March 2, 1954.

Means for making metallized electrical condensers. 2,683,792. July 13, 1954.

Process and apparatus for soldering. 2,696,546. December 7, 1954.

Means and method of manufacturing electrical condensers. 2,716,180. August 23, 1955.

Manufacture of electrical capacitors. 2,769,889. November 6, 1956.

Electronic speed light. 2,775,718. December 25, 1956.

Variable electrical capacitors. 2,881,372. April 7, 1959. [With I. Rossi and M. H. Dubilier.]

Electrical suppressor. 2,884,605. April 28, 1959.

Cold pressure welding. 2,894,321. July 14, 1959.

Method for manufacturing electrical condensers. 2,910,764. November 3, 1959.

Means and method of manufacturing metallized electrical capacitors. 2,913,647. November 17, 1959.

Capacitor tab insertion. 3,018,064. January 23, 1962.

Relaxer device. 3,173,419. March 16, 1965. [With E. G. Cotton.]

Dual-film metallized condensers. 3,179,862. April 20, 1965.

Wound-paper capacitors and manufacturing method and apparatus. 3,198,934. August 3, 1965.

Automatic impact assembly. 3,230,781. January 25, 1966.

Capacitor and method of adjusting the same. 3,258,666. June
28, 1966.

Title Index

Dual-film metallized condensers. 3,179,862.
Electric condenser. 2,075,891.
Electric flasher device. 1,692,292.
Electric heater. 1,079,225.
Electric sadiron. 1,757,658.
Electric switch. 2,284,644.
Electrical apparatus. 1,485,462.
Electrical capacitor. 2,398,417.
Electrical condenser. 1,391,672; 1,455,781; 1,497,095;
    1,526,664; 1,537,660; 1,571,512; 1,575,044; 1,575,045;
    1,627,493; 1,671,519; 1,688,960; 1,688,961; 1,710,412;
    1,713,867; 1,731,653; 1,742,759; 1,754,268; 1,757,657;
    1,768,441; 1,768,442; 1,816,640; 1,816,641; 1,821,055;
    1,824,805; 1,824,806; 1,829,891; 1,833,392; 1,836,707;
    1,862,302; 1,870,797; 1,870,950; 2,043,532; 2,128,990;
    2,133,086.
Electrical condenser. Design 70,547. July 13, 1926.
Electrical condenser. Design 70,548. July 13, 1926.
Electrical condenser for ignition circuits. 1,541,630.
Electrical condenser unit. 1,870,948.
Electrical-discharge-producing device. 1,307,854.
Electrical liquid treating device. 2,532,016.
Electrical resistance. 1,694,167.
Electrical structure. 1,628,627; 1,759,230; 1,874,936.
Electrical suppressor. 2,884,605.
Electrode device for high-frequency apparatus. 1,121,077.
Electrolytic condenser. 2,243,814.
Electromagnetic operating mechanism. 2,023,355.
Electronic speed light. 2,775,718.
Electrostatic condenser. 1,731,652.
Fastening device, particularly rivets. 2,238,463.
Flasher device. 1,898,174.
Flexible track system for toy trains. 2,565,359.
Grid leak and condenser. 1,744,301.
Grid-leak resistance. 1,683,067.
Hearing aid. 2,566,761.

Hearing aid amplifier. 2,257,840.
Hearing aid system. 2,321,370.
High tension generator. 2,038,553; 2,047,463.
High-frequency apparatus. 1,004,152; 1,023,135.
High frequency small capacity condenser. 1,937,010.
High-potential condenser. 1,639,650; 1,744,454.
High-voltage terminal. 2,450,273.
Indicating device for high frequency currents. 1,802,077.
Insect screen. 2,278,538.
Insulating structure for high-potential condenser terminals and
    the like. 1,650,983.
Insulating structure for high-potential condensers. 1,565,799.
Insulation-testing device. 1,334,141.
Lamp socket. 1,779,804.
Loud-speaker. 1,755,636.
Magnetic lock. 2,288,688.
Making electrical condensers. 1,926,842; 2,143,369.
Manufacture of electrical capacitors. 2,769,889.
Means and method of manufacturing electrical condensers.
    2,716,180.
Means and method of manufacturing metallized electrical
    capacitors. 2,913,647.
Means for making metallized electrical condensers. 2,683,792.
Means for manufacturing metallized electrical capacitors.
    2,671,157.
Method and apparatus for interrupting electrical circuits.
    1,623,531.
Method for manufacturing electrical condensers. 2,910,764.
Mousetrap. 1,630,241.
Multifrequency generator. 1,477,271.
Playing card container. 2,577,007.
Power factor condenser. 1,842,374.
Power tractor condenser. 1,945,108.
Process and apparatus for making electric condensers.
    1,785,479.
Process and apparatus for soldering. 2,696,546.

Protective unit. 1,281,309.
Purse and like container. 2,288,996.
Radio appliance. 1,705,559.
Radiosignaling apparatus. 1,382,177.
Razor holder. 1,475,940.
Relaxer device. 3,173,419.
Rolled condenser. 1,870,949.
Screen or webbing material. 2,355,635.
Self-protecting condenser. 1,350,010.
Series condenser. 1,327,593.
Snap switch. 2,341,858.
Spark plug. 1,729,248.
Support for resistances. 1,740,160.
System for controlling knitting. 2,199,336.
Telephone receiver. 1,602,814.
Terminal construction. 2,374,084.
Terminal connection for condensers. 1,480,604.
Thermoplastic belt. 2,445,889.
Thermostatic switch. 2,288,517.
Track system for toy trains. 2,196,257.
Tube reviver. 1,698,625.
Variable condenser. 1,396,030; 1,429,277; 1,646,236;
    1,705,242; 1,714,662; 1,722,326; 1,735,532; 1,740,159;
    1,750,393; 1,756,512; 1,763,554; 1,841,095.
Variable electrical capacitors. 2,881,372.
Variometer. 1,861,052.
Wired radio communication system. 1,944,226.
Wireless apparatus and method therefor. 1,279,850.
Wound-paper capacitors and manufacturing method and
    apparatus. 3,198,934.

ALLEN B. DU MONT (1901-1965)

[Note: Patents assigned to Allen B. Du Mont Laboratories but not in Du Mont's name are not listed.]

Mount for radiotubes. 1,719,968. July 9, 1929.

Apparatus and method for testing electrical devices. 1,814,437. July 14, 1931.

Sound operated circuit controller. 1,844,117. February 9, 1932.

Multiple electrode radiotron. 1,857,589. May 10, 1932. [With P. T. Weeks.]

Radiotube. 1,898,351. February 21, 1933.

Ultra-high frequency generating system. 1,915,356. June 27, 1933.

Automatic testing apparatus. 1,916,364. July 4, 1933.

Filament. 1,924,543. August 29, 1933.

Rectifier device. 1,924,544. August 29, 1933.

Automatic aging and testing method and mechanism. 1,955,794. April 24, 1934. [With R. M. Zimber.]

Cathode ray instrument for measuring electrical quantities. 1,960,333. May 29, 1934.

Exhaust machine. 1,967,571. July 24, 1934. [With R. M. Zimber.]

Television system. 1,984,673. December 18, 1934.

Electron turbine. 1,999,407. April 30, 1935.

Teltautograph. 2,000,014. May 7, 1935.

Voltmeter for vacuum tubes. 2,014,106. September 10, 1935.

Synchronous electron motor. 2,067,382. January 12, 1937.

Current generator and converter. 2,082,327. June 1, 1937.

Commutating device. 2,085,576. June 29, 1937.

Cathode ray tube. 2,087,280. July 20, 1937.

Cathode ray device. 2,098,231. November 9, 1937.

Cathautograph. 2,185,705. January 2, 1940.

Method and system for television communication. 2,186,634. January 9, 1940.

Cathode ray tube. 2,186,635. January 9, 1940.

Television transmitting system. 2,207,048. July 9, 1940. [With Richard L. Campbell.]

Synchronizing generator. 2,209,507. July 30, 1940. [With Richard L. Campbell.]

Cathode ray tube. 2,225,099. December 17, 1940. [With Peter S. Christaldi.]

Cathode-ray tube control device for television scanning apparatus. 2,229,556. January 21, 1941. [With T. T. Goldsmith, Jr.]

Monitoring and control system. 2,297,752. October 6, 1942. [With T. T. Goldsmith.]

Method and system for television communication. 2,299,471. October 20, 1942. [With T. T. Goldsmith.]

System for color television receivers. 2,337,980. December 28, 1943. [With T. T. Goldsmith.]

Photovision. 2,472,889. June 14, 1949.

Projection screen. 2,521,571. September 5, 1950. [With T. T. Goldsmith.]

Adjacent area illuminator for cathode-ray tubes. 2,669,708. February 16, 1954.

Dual image viewing apparatus. 2,832,821. April 29, 1958.

Title Index

Cathode ray tube. 2,087,280; 2,186,635; 2,225,099.
Cathode ray device. 2,098,231.
Cathode ray instrument for measuring electrical quantities.
    1,960,333.
Cathode-ray tube control device for television scanning
    apparatus. 2,229,556.
Commutating device. 2,085,576.
Current generator and converter. 2,082,327.
Dual image viewing apparatus. 2,832,821.
Electron turbine. 1,999, 407.
Exhaust machine. 1,967,571.
"Eye" tube. *See* 2,098,231.
Filament. 1,924,543.
"Magic eye" tube. *See* 2,098,231.
Method and system for television communication. 2,186,634;
    2,299,471.
Monitoring and control system. 2,297,752.
Mount for radiotubes. 1,719,968.
Multiple electrode radiotron. 1,857,589.
Photovision. 2,472,889.
Projection screen. 2,521,571.
Radiotube. 1,898,351.
Rectifier device. 1,924,544.
Sound operated circuit controller. 1,844,117.
Synchronizing generator. 2,209,507.
Synchronous electron motor. 2,067,382.
System for color television receivers. 2,337,980.
Television system. 1,984,673.
Television transmitting system. 2,207,048.
Teltautograph. 2,000,014.
Ultra-high frequency generating system. 1,915,356.
Voltmeter for vacuum tubes. 2,014,106.

PHILO T. FARNSWORTH (1906-1971)

[Note: Patents assigned to Farnsworth Television and Radio Corporation but not in Farnsworth's name are not listed.]

Electric oscillator system. 1,758,359. May 13, 1930.

Television system. 1,773,980. August 26, 1930.

Television receiving system. 1,773,981. August 26, 1930.

Light valve. 1,806,935. May 26, 1931.

Synchronizing system. 1,844,949. February 16, 1932.

Dissector target. 1,941,344. December 26, 1933.

Electron multiplier. 1,969,399. August 7, 1934.

Photoelectric apparatus. 1,970,036. August 14, 1934.

Thermionic vacuum tube. 1,975,143. October 2, 1934.

Electrical discharge apparatus. 1,986,330. January 1, 1935.

Admittance neutralizing amplifier. 1,986,331. January 1, 1935.

System of pulse transmission. 2,026,379. December 31, 1935.

Method and apparatus for television. 2,037,711. April 21, 1936.

Scanning and synchronizing system. 2,051,372. August 18, 1936.

Slope wave generator. 2,059,219. November 3, 1936.

Scanning oscillator. 2,059,683. November 3, 1936.

Incandescent light source. 2,066,070. December 29, 1936.

Electron multiplying device. 2,071,515. February 23, 1937.

Oscillation generator. 2,071,516. February 23, 1937.

Multipactor phase control. 2,071,517. February 23, 1937.

Electron image amplifier. 2,085,742. July 6, 1937.

Image dissector. 2,087,683. July 20, 1937.

Incandescent light source. 2,089,054. August 3, 1937.

Multipactor oscillator and amplifier. 2,091,439. August 31, 1937.

Projection apparatus. 2,091,705. August 31, 1937.

Luminescent screen. 2,098,000. November 2, 1937.

Thermionic oscillograph. 2,099,846. November 23, 1937.

Image analysis tube. 2,100,841. November 30, 1937.

Charge storage tube. 2,100,842. November 30, 1937.

Luminescent screen and use. 2,104,253. January 4, 1938.

Radiation frequency converter. 2,107,782. February 8, 1938. [With D. K. Lippincott.]

High power projection oscillograph. 2,109,289. February 22, 1938. [With F. J. Somers.]

Image receiving tube. 2,118,186. May 24, 1938.

Electron multiplier. Reissue 20,759. June 14, 1938.

Beam scanning dissector. 2,124,057. July 19, 1938.

Operating electron multipliers. 2,128,580. August 20, 1938.

Multipactor. 2,135,615. November 8, 1938.

Multipactor oscillator. 2,137,528. November 22, 1938.

Secondary emission electrode. 2,139,813. December 13, 1938

Cathode ray tube. 2,139,814. December 13, 1938.

Projecting oscillight. 2,140,284. December 13, 1938.

Multiplier coupling system. 2,140,285. December 13, 1938.

Charge storage dissector. 2,140,695. December 20, 1938.

Controlling electron multipliers. 2,140,832. December 20, 1938.

Charge storage dissector tube. 2,141,836. December 27, 1938.

Multistage multipactor. 2,141,837. December 27, 1938.

Split cathode multiplier tube. 2,141,838. December 27, 1938.

Projection means. 2,143,145. January 10, 1939.

Repeater. 2,143,146. January 10, 1939. [With R. L. Snyder.]

Electron multiplication. 2,143,262. January 10, 1939.

Cathode ray tube. 2,149,045. February 28, 1939.

Dissector tube. 2,153,918. April 11, 1939.

Producing incandescent images. 2,155,478. April 25, 1939.
[With H. S. Bamford.]

Means and method for transmitting synchronizing pulses in
television. 2,155,479. April 25, 1939.

Detector. 2,156,807. May 2, 1939.

Cathode ray tube. 2,158,279. May 16, 1939.

Absorption oscillator. 2,159,521. May 23, 1939.

Two-stage electron multiplier. 2,161,620. June 6, 1939.

Television method. 2,168,768. August 8, 1939.

Radio frequency multipactor amplifier. 2,172,152. September
5, 1939.

Self-energized alternating current multiplier. 2,174,487.
September 26, 1939.

Oscillator. 2,174,488. September 26, 1939.

Producing an incandescent image. 2,179,086. November 7, 1939.

Electron multiplier. 2,179,996. November 14, 1939.

Operating electron multipliers. 2,180,279. November 14, 1939.

Cold cathode electron discharge tube. 2,184,910. December 26, 1939.

Diode oscillator tube construction. 2,189,358. February 6, 1940.

Producing electron multiplication. 2,204,479. June 11, 1940.

Image dissector. Reissue 21,504. July 9, 1940.

Scanning current generator. 2,214,077. September 10, 1940.

Two-stage oscillograph. 2,216,266. October 1, 1940.

Split cathode multiplier. 2,217,860. October 15, 1940.

Image source. 2,213,070. August 27, 1940.

Means and method of image analysis. 2,216,264. October 1, 1940.

Image dissector. 2,216,265. October 1, 1940.

X-ray projection device. 2,221,374. November 12, 1940.

Amplifier. 2,221,473. November 12, 1940.

High efficiency amplifier. 2,223,001. November 26, 1940.

Shielded anode electron multiplier. 2,203,048. June 4, 1940. [With R. L. Snyder.]

Cathode ray amplifier. 2,228,388. January 14, 1941.

Image projector. 2,233,887. March 4, 1941.

Charge storage amplifier. 2,233,888. March 4, 1941.

Dissector tube. 2,235,477. March 18, 1941.

Electronic amplifier. 2,239,149. April 22, 1941.

Television scanning and synchronizing system. 2,246,625. June 24, 1941.

Cathode ray amplifying tube. 2,251,124. July 29, 1941.

Image analyzing system. 2,254,140. August 26, 1941.

Image amplifier. 2,257,942. October 7, 1941.

Electron multiplier. 2,260,613. October 28, 1941.

Cold cathode electron discharge tube. 2,263,032. November 18, 1941.

Dissector tube. 2,264,630. December 2, 1941.

Electron image amplifier. Reissue 22,009. January 20, 1942.

Apparatus for and electron discharge control. 2,274,194. February 24, 1942.

Scanning means and method. 2,280,572. April 21, 1942.

Electron control device. 2,286,076. June 9, 1942.

Manufacturing cathode-ray targets. 2,286,478. June 16, 1942.

Rectifier. 2,287,607. June 23, 1942.

Image amplifier. 2,291,577. July 28, 1942.

Image dissector. 2,292,111. August 4, 1942.

Electron image amplifier. 2,292,437. August 11, 1942.

Deflecting system. 2,297,949. October 6, 1942.

Cathode ray signal reproducing tube. 2,301,388. November 10, 1942.

Electric recording and reproducing system. 2,304,633. December 8, 1942.

Electron control device. 2,311,981. February 23, 1943.

Television projection system. 2,315,113. March 30, 1943.

Image reproducing device. 2,355,212. August 8, 1944.

Television image analyzing tube. 2,641,723. June 9, 1953.

Cathode ray tube and system. 2,754,449. July 10, 1956.

Storage type electron tube systems. 2,830,111. April 8, 1958.

Color television apparatus. 2,921,228. January 12, 1960.

Cathode ray tube. 2,941,100. June 14, 1960.

Color television receiver. 2,951,113. August 30, 1960.

Light translating device. 2,992,346. July 11, 1961.

Radiation translating device. 2,992,358. July 11, 1961.

Electron image-discharge device. 3,108,202. October 22, 1963.

Transducing apparatus. 3,073,899. January 15, 1963.

Ion transport vacuum pump. 3,181,028. April 27, 1965.

Electron gun in the form of a multipactor. 3,201,640. August 17, 1965.

Ion transport pump. 3,240,421. March 15, 1966.

Electric discharge device for producing interactions between nuclei. 3,258,402. June 28, 1966.

Process and apparatus for drying and treating lumber. 3,283,412. November 8, 1966.

Microwave amplifier utilizing multipaction to produce periodically bunched electrons. 3,312,857. April 4, 1967.

Method and apparatus for producing nuclear-fusion reactions. 3,386,883. June 4, 1968.

Lumber drying. 3,574,949. April 13, 1971. [With Frederick R. Furth.]

Title Index

Absorption oscillator. 2,159,521.

Admittance neutralizing amplifier. 1,986,331.

Amplifier. 2,221,473.

Apparatus for and electron discharge control. 2,274,194.

Beam scanning dissector. 2,124,057.

Cathode ray amplifier. 2,228,388.

Cathode ray amplifying tube. 2,251,124.

Cathode ray tube. 2,139,814; 2,149,045; 2,158,279;
    2,941,100.

Cathode ray tube and system. 2,754,449.

Cathode ray signal reproducing tube. 2,301,388.

Charge storage amplifier. 2,233,888.

Charge storage dissector. 2,140,695.

Charge storage dissector tube. 2,141,836.

Charge storage tube. 2,100,842.

Cold cathode electron discharge tube. 2,184,910; 2,263,032.

Color television apparatus. 2,921,228.

Color television receiver. 2,951,113.

Controlling electron multipliers. 2,140,832.

Deflecting system. 2,297,949.

Detector. 2,156,807.

Diode oscillator tube construction. 2,189,358.

Dissector tube. 2,153,918; 2,235,477; 2,264,630.

Dissector target. 1,941,344.

Electric discharge device for producing interactions between
    nuclei. 3,258,402.

Electric oscillator system. 1,758,359.

Electric recording and reproducing system. 2,304,633.

Electrical discharge apparatus. 1,986,330.

Electron control device. 2,286,076; 2,311,981.

Electron gun in the form of a multipactor. 3,201,640.

Electron image amplifier. 2,085,742; 2,292,437.

Electron image amplifier. Reissue 22,009. January 20, 1942.

Electron image-discharge device. 3,108,202.

Electron multiplication. 2,143,262.

Electron multiplier. 1,969,399; 2,179,996; 2,260,613.

Electron multiplier. Reissue 20,759. June 14, 1938.

Electron multiplying device. 2,071,515.

Electronic amplifier. 2,239,149.

High efficiency amplifier. 2,223,001.

High power projection oscillograph. 2,109,289.

Image amplifier. 2,257,942; 2,291,577.

Image analysis tube. 2,100,841.

Image analyzing system. 2,254,140.

Image dissector. 2,087,683; 2,216,265; 2,292,111.

Image dissector. Reissue 21,504. July 9, 1940.

Image projector. 2,233,887.

Image receiving tube. 2,118,186.

Image reproducing device. 2,355,212.

Image source. 2,213,070.

Incandescent light source. 2,066,070; 2,089,054.

Ion transport pump. 3,240,421.

Ion transport vacuum pump. 3,181,028.

Light translating device. 2,992,346.

Light valve. 1,806,935.

Lumber drying. 3,574,949.

Luminescent screen. 2,098,000.

Luminescent screen and use. 2,104,253.

Manufacturing cathode-ray targets. 2,286,478.

Means and method for transmitting synchronizing pulses in television. 2,155,479.

Means and method of image analysis. 2,216,264.

Method and apparatus for producing nuclear-fusion reactions. 3,386,883.

Method and apparatus for television. 2,037,711.

Microwave amplifier utilizing multipaction to produce periodically bunched electrons. 3,312,857.

Multipactor. 2,135,615.

Multipactor oscillator. 2,137,528.

Multipactor oscillator and amplifier. 2,091,439.

Multipactor phase control. 2,071,517.
Multiplier coupling system. 2,140,285.
Multistage multipactor. 2,141,837.
Operating electron multipliers. 2,128,580; 2,180,279.
Oscillation generator. 2,071,516.
Oscillator. 2,174,488.
Photoelectric apparatus. 1,970,036.
Process and apparatus for drying and treating lumber.
    3,283,412.
Producing an incandescent image. 2,179,086.
Producing electron multiplication. 2,204,479.
Producing incandescent images. 2,155,478.
Projecting oscillight. 2,140,284.
Projection apparatus. 2,091,705.
Projection means. 2,143,145.
Radiation frequency converter. 2,107,782.
Radiation translating device. 2,992,358.
Radio frequency multipactor amplifier. 2,172,152.
Rectifier. 2,287,607.
Repeater. 2,143,146.
Scanning and synchronizing system. 2,051,372.
Scanning current generator. 2,214,077.
Scanning means and method. 2,280,572.
Scanning oscillator. 2,059,683.
Secondary emission electrode. 2,139,813.
Self-energized alternating current multiplier. 2,174,487.
Shielded anode electron multiplier. 2,203,048.
Slope wave generator. 2,059,219.
Split cathode multiplier. 2,217,860.
Split cathode multiplier tube. 2,141,838.
Storage type electron tube systems. 2,830,111.
Synchronizing system. 1,844,949.
System of pulse transmission. 2,026,379.
Television image analyzing tube. 2,641,723.
Television method. 2,168,768.
Television projection system. 2,315,113.

Television receiving system. 1,773,981.
Television scanning and synchronizing system. 2,246,625.
Television system. 1,773,980.
Thermionic oscillograph. 2,099,846.
Thermionic vacuum tube. 1,975,143.
Transducing apparatus. 3,073,899.
Two-stage electron multiplier. 2,161,620.
Two-stage oscillograph. 2,216,266.
X-ray projection device. 2,221,374.

REGINALD A. FESSENDEN (1866-1932)

Leading-in wire for incandescent lamps. 452,494. May 19, 1891. 55:912.

Manufacture of incandescent electric lamps. 453,742. June 9, 1891. 55:1324.

Molding for electrical conductors. 506,311. October 10, 1893. 65:179.

Pencil for incandescent lamps. 638,837. December 12, 1899. 89:2123. [With G. McCargo.]

Pencil for incandescent lamps. 638,838. December 12, 1899. 89:2123. [With G. McCargo.]

Incandescent lamp. 638,839. December 12, 1899. 89:2123. [With G. McCargo.]

Incandescent lamp. 638,840. December 12, 1899. 89:2123. [With G. McCargo.]

Incandescent lamp. 639,161. December 12, 1899. 89:2231. [With G. McCargo.]

Induction-coil for X-ray apparatus. 644,972. March 6, 1900. 90:1907.

X-ray apparatus. 648,660. May 1, 1900. 91:933.

Incandescent lamp. 650,531. May 29, 1900. 91:1684. [With G. McCargo.]

Induction-coil. 654,390. July 24, 1900. 92:708.

Incandescent lamp. 670,316. March 19, 1901. 94:2306.

Wireless telegraphy. 706,735. August 12, 1902. 100:1420.

Apparatus for wireless telegraphy. 706,736. August 12, 1902. 100:1421.

Wireless telegraphy. 706,737. August 12, 1902. 100:1422.

Wireless telegraphy. 706,738. August 12, 1902. 100:1423.

Conductor for wireless telegraphy. 706,739. August 12, 1902. 100:1423.

Wireless signaling. 706,740. August 12, 1902. 100:1424.

Apparatus for wireless telegraphy. 706,741. August 12, 1902. 100:1424.

Wireless signaling. 706,742. August 12, 1902. 100:1425.

Wireless signaling. 706,743. August 12, 1902. 100:1426.

Current-actuated wave-responsive device. 706,744. August 12, 1902. 100:1426.

Signaling by electromagnetic waves. 706,745. August 12, 1902. 100:1426.

Signaling by electromagnetic waves. 706,746. August 12, 1902. 100:1427.

Apparatus for signaling by electromagnetic waves. 706,747. August 12, 1902. 100:1428.

Current-operated receiver for electromagnetic waves. 715,043. December 2, 1902. 101:1990.

Selective signaling by electromagnetic waves. 715,203. December 2, 1902. 101:2053.

Transmission and receipt of signals. 727,325. May 5, 1903. 104:203.

Selective signaling by electromagnetic waves. 727,326. May 5, 1903. 104:204.

Receiver for electromagnetic waves. 727,327. May 5, 1903. 104:205.

Receiver for signaling. 727,328. May 5, 1903. 104:205.

Signaling by electromagnetic waves. 727,329. May 5, 1903. 104:205.

Signaling by electromagnetic waves. 727,330. May 5, 1903. 104:206.

Receiver for electromagnetic waves. 727,331. May 5, 1903. 104:206.

Receiver for electromagnetic waves. Reissue 12,115. May 26, 1903. 104:1108.

Signaling by electromagnetic waves. 730,753. June 9, 1903. 104:1606.

Utilizing the energy of waves. 731,029. June 16, 1903. 104:1734.

Signaling by electromagnetic waves. 742,779. October 27, 1903. 106:2260.

Signaling by electromagnetic waves. 742,780. October 27, 1903. 106:2260.

Wireless telegraphy. Reissue 12,168. November 10, 1903. 107:529. [With D. S. Wolcott.]

Wireless telegraphy. Reissue 12,169. November 10, 1903. 107:530.

Selective signaling. 752,894. February 23, 1904. 108:1985.

Signaling by electromagnetic waves. 752,895. February 23, 1904. 108:1985.

Wireless signaling. 753,863. March 8, 1904. 109:300.

Signaling by electromagnetic waves. 753,864. March 8, 1904. 109:301.

Signaling by electromagnetic waves. 754,058. March 8, 1904. 109:385.

Apparatus for transmitting and receiving signals. 777,014. December 6, 1904. 113:1672.

Capacity. 793,647. July 4, 1905. 117:9.

Receiver for electromagnetic waves. 793,648. July 4, 1905. 117:9.

Signaling by electromagnetic waves. 793,649. July 4, 1905. 117:10.

Signaling by electromagnetic waves. 793,650. July 4, 1905. 117:11.

Aerial for wireless signaling. 793,651. July 4, 1905. 117:11.

Signaling by electromagnetic waves. 793,652. July 4, 1905. 117:11.

Wireless telegraphy. 793,718. July 4, 1905. 117:40.

Condenser. 793,777. July 4, 1905. 117:68.

Capacity. 814,951. March 13, 1906. 121:467.

Wireless telegraphy. 897,278. September 1, 1908. 136:7.

Means for generating high-frequency electric oscillations. 897,279. September 1, 1908. 136:7.

Electric signaling. 915,280. March 16, 1909. 140:586.

Signaling. 916,428. March 30, 1909. 140:1017.

Receiver for electromagnetic waves. 916,429. March 30, 1909. 140:1018.

Detecting device for wireless telegraphy. 917,574. April 6, 1909. 141:209.

Wireless signaling. 918,306. April 13, 1909. 141:484.

Apparatus for wireless signaling. 918,307. April 13, 1909. 141:484.

Receiver for electromagnetic waves. 921,531. May 11, 1909.
142:506.

Wireless telegraphy. 923,962. June 8, 1909. 143:318.

Wireless telegraphy. 923,963. June 8, 1909. 143:318.

Signaling by electromagnetic waves. 928,371. July 20, 1909.
144:617.

Producing high-frequency oscillations. 932,111. August 24,
1909. 145:902.

Lightning-arrester. 932,112. August 24, 1909. 145:902.

Means for cleaning guns. 938,836. November 2, 1909.
148:133.

Determining positions of vessels. 941,565. November 30,
1909. 148:1163.

Wireless telegraphy. 948,068. February 1, 1910. 151:98.

Signaling by electromagnetic waves. 956,489. April 26, 1910.
153:1054.

Wireless signaling. 960,631. June 7, 1910. 155:132.

Electric signaling. 962,014. June 21, 1910. 155:648.

Receiver for electric signaling. 962,015. June 21, 1910.
155:648.

Receiver for electromagnetic waves. 962,016. June 21, 1910.
155:649.

Electrical apparatus. 962,017. June 21, 1910. 155:649.

Method of signaling. 962,018. June 21, 1910. 155:649.

Wireless telegraphy. 974,762. November 1, 1910. 160:238.

Transmission and receipt of electrical energy. 979,144.
December 20, 1910. 161:651.

Electrical signaling. 979,145. December 20, 1910. 161:652.

Multiplex telegraphy. 981,406. January 10, 1911. 162:456.

Signaling by electromagnetic waves. 998,567. July 18, 1911.
168:754.

Signaling by electromagnetic waves. 1,002,049. August 29,
1911. 169:1102.

Receiver for signaling. 1,002,050. August 29, 1911.
169:1103.

Signaling by electromagnetic waves. 1,002,051. August 29,
1911. 169:1103.

Electrical signaling. 1,002,052. August 29, 1911. 169:1103.

Determining position of vessels. 1,002,141. August 29, 1911.
169:1132.

Means for transmission of energy by electromagnetic waves.
1,015,881. January 30, 1912. 174:1070.

Signaling. 1,019,236. March 5, 1912. 176:80.

Signaling by electromagnetic waves. 1,020,032. March 12, 1912. 176:376.

Receiver for electromagnetic waves. 1,022,539. April 9, 1912. 177:294.

Wireless signaling. 1,022,540. April 9, 1912. 177:294.

Determining frequency of periodic impulses. 1,022,584. April 9, 1912. 177:309.

Wireless telegraphy. 1,035,334. August 13, 1912. 181:345.

High-frequency electrical conductor. 1,039,717. October 1, 1912. 183:16.

Receiver for electromagnetic waves. 1,042,778. October 29, 1912. 183:1182.

Receiving electromagnetic waves. 1,044,637. November 19, 1912. 184:615.

Wireless telegraphy. 1,045,781. November 26, 1912. 184:1045.

Wireless telegraphy. 1,045,782. November 26, 1912. 184:1045.

Contact for electromagnetic mechanism. 1,048,670. December 31, 1912. 185:1131. [With H. M. Barrett and S.M. Kintner.]

Electric signaling apparatus. 1,050,441. January 14, 1913. 186:417. [With S. M. Kintner and H. M. Barrett.]

Signaling. 1,050,728. January 14, 1913. 186:512. [With S. M. Kintner and H. M. Barrett.]

Wireless telegraphy. 1,059,665. April 22, 1913. 189:898. [With S. M. Kintner and H. M. Barrett.]

Apparatus for wireless signaling. 1,059,666. April 22, 1913. 189:898. [With S. M. Kintner and H. M. Barrett.]

Wireless signaling. 1,074,423. September 30, 1913. 194:1064.

Magnetic material. 1,074,424. September 30, 1913. 194:1064. [With S. M. Kintner and H. M. Barrett.]

Signaling by electromagnetic waves. 1,080,271. December 2, 1913. 197:124. [With S. M. Kintner and H. M. Barrett.]

Apparatus for electric signaling. 1,101,914. June 30, 1914. 203:1404. [With S. M. Kintner and H. M. Barrett.]

Wireless signaling. 1,101,915. June 30, 1914. 203:1405. [With S. M. Kintner and H. M. Barrett.]

Signaling by sound and other longitudinal elastic impulses. 1,108,895. September 1, 1914. 206:11.

System of storing power. 1,112,441. October 6, 1914. 207:9.

Storage and care of wheeled vehicles. 1,114,975. October 27, 1914. 207:1033.

Agricultural engineering. 1,121,722. December 22, 1914. 209:1102.

Sending mechanism for electromagnetic waves. 1,126,966. February 2, 1915. 211:105. [With S. M. Kintner and H. M. Barrett.]

Apparatus for converting heat into work. 1,132,465. March 16, 1915. 212:992.

Electric signaling. 1,132,568. March 23, 1915. 212:1077. [With S. M. Kintner and H. M. Barrett.]

Wireless telegraphy. 1,132,569. March 23, 1915. 212:1077. [With S. M. Kintner and H. M. Barrett.]

Method of and apparatus for reproducing impulses. 1,133,435. March 30, 1915. 212:1428.

Transmitting and receiving electrical energy. 1,141,386. June 1, 1915. 215:108. [With S. M. Kintner and H. M. Barrett.]

Apparatus for the transmission and receipt of electrical energy. 1,141,453. June 1, 1915. 215:131. [With S. M. Kintner and H. M. Barrett.]

Wireless telegraphy. 1,147,010. July 20, 1915. 216:753. [With S. M. Kintner and H. M. Barrett.]

Amplifying electrical impulses. 1,154,750. September 28, 1915. 218:936.

Apparatus for the transmission of energy by electric oscillations. 1,156,677. October 12, 1915. 219:497. [With S. M. Kintner and H. M. Barrett.]

Transmitting and receiving signals. 1,157,094. October 19, 1915. 219:673. [With S. M. Kintner and H. M. Barrett.]

Apparatus for generating and receiving electromagnetic waves. 1,158,123. October 26, 1915. 219:1097. [With S. M. Kintner and H. M. Barrett.]

Signaling apparatus for aerial navigation. 1,158,124. October 26, 1915. 219:1097. [With S. M. Kintner and H. M. Barrett.]

Apparatus for wireless signaling. 1,165,862. December 28, 1915. 221:1217. [With S. M. Kintner and H. M. Barrett.]

Apparatus for producing high-frequency oscillations. 1,166,892. January 4, 1916. 222:167. [With S. M. Kintner and H. M. Barrett.]

Producing high-frequency oscillations. 1,166,893. January 4, 1916. 222:168.

Dynamo-electric machinery. 1,167,366. January 4, 1916. 222:334.

Means of transmitting intelligence. 1,170,969. February 8, 1916. 223:458. [With S. M. Kintner and H. M. Barrett.]

Transmitting energy by electromagnetic waves. 1,172,017. February 15, 1916. 223:875. [With S. M. Kintner and H. M. Barrett.]

Electromagnetic indicator. 1,172,018. February 15, 1916. 223:875. [With S. M. Kintner and H. M. Barrett.]

Wireless telegraphy. 1,175,418. March 14, 1916. 224:530. [With S. M. Kintner and H. M. Barrett.]

Wireless signaling. 1,176,282. March 21, 1916. 224:872. [With S. M. Kintner and H. M. Barrett.]

Wireless signaling. 1,178,507. April 11, 1916. 225:385. [With S. M. Kintner and H. M. Barrett.]

Electric signaling. 1,179,906. April 18, 1916. 225:932. [With S. M. Kintner and H. M. Barrett.]

Signaling by electromagnetic waves. 1,182,003. May 9, 1916. 226:353. [With S. M. Kintner and H. M. Barrett.]

Signaling. 1,182,843. May 9, 1916. 226:646.

Signaling by electromagnetic waves. 1,184,843. May 30, 1916. 226:1485.

Utilizing pulverulent matter as fuel. 1,191,072. July 11, 1916. 228:701.

Method and apparatus for amplifying electric impulses. 1,196,938. September 5, 1916. 230:72. [With L. Cohen, S. M. Kintner, and H. M. Barrett.]

Apparatus and method for producing vibratory motions. 1,207,387. December 5, 1916. 233:208.

Method and apparatus for submarine signaling. 1,207,388. December 5, 1916. 233:208.

Submarine, subterranean, and aerial telephony. 1,212,202. January 16, 1917. 234:690.

Apparatus for phonograph-kinetoscopes. 1,213,176. January 23, 1917. 234:1067.

Dynamo-electric machinery. 1,213,610. January 23, 1917. 234:1219.

Dynamo-electric machinery. 1,213,611. January 23, 1917. 234:1219.

Power generation. 1,214,531. February 6, 1917. 235:17.

Power plant. 1,217,165. February 27, 1917. 235:1072.

Measuring distance. 1,217,585. February 27, 1917. 235:1220.

Method and apparatus for locating ore-bodies. 1,240,328. September 18, 1917. 242:576.

System of storing power. 1,247,520. November 20, 1917. 244:768.

Method and apparatus for producing alternating currents. 1,265,068. May 7, 1918. 250:55.

Gun-sight. 1,265,766. May 14, 1918. 250:275.

Method and apparatus for agricultural engineering. 1,268,949. June 11, 1918. 251:266.

Method and apparatus for transmitting and receiving sound-waves through ground. 1,270,398. June 25, 1918. 251:721.

Sound-producer. 1,277,562. September 3, 1918. 254:63.

Apparatus for submarines. 1,291,458. January 14, 1919. 258:368.

Method of and apparatus for heat insulation. 1,301,675. April 22, 1919. 261:751.

Submarine signaling. 1,311,157. July 29, 1919. 264:710.

Submarine signaling. 1,318,739. October 14, 1919. 267:267.

Method of and apparatus for obtaining increased circulation. 1,318,740. October 14, 1919. 267:267.

Detecting and locating ships. 1,319,145. October 21, 1919. 267:371.

Method and apparatus for eliminating undesired vibrations. 1,319,521. October 21, 1919. 267:442.

Method and apparatus for cooling and lubricating systems. 1,331,907. February 24, 1920. 271:601.

Locating enemy-gun positions. 1,341,795. June 1, 1920. 275:36.

Apparatus for submarine signaling. 1,348,556. August 3, 1920. 277:83.

Method and apparatus for detecting low-frequency impulses. 1,348,825. August 3, 1920. 277:133.

Method and apparatus for submarine signaling and detection. 1,348,826. August 3, 1920. 277:133.

Method and apparatus for submarine signaling. 1,348,827. August 3, 1920. 277:133.

Method and apparatus for sound insulation. 1,348,828. August 3, 1920. 277:134.

Method and apparatus for locating submarines. 1,348,855. August 10, 1920. 277:192.

Apparatus for directive signaling. 1,348,856. August 10, 1920. 277:192.

Apparatus for directive signaling. 1,355,598. October 12, 1920. 279:279.

Artificial-leather article. 1,357,449. November 2, 1920. 280:47.

Wheel-puller. 1,357,698. November 2, 1920. 280:94.

Wireless direction-finder. 1,374,293. April 12, 1921. 285:218.

Destroying enemy gun positions. 1,383,219. June 28, 1921. 287:711.

Method and apparatus for signaling and otherwise utilizing radiant impulses. 1,384,014. July 5, 1921. 288:157.

Sound signaling. 1,384,029. July 5, 1921. 288:160.

Destroying enemy gun positions. 1,384,030. July 5, 1921. 288:160.

Submarine signaling. 1,394,482. October 18, 1921.

Method and apparatus for submarine signaling. 1,394,483. October 18, 1921.

Method and apparatus for submarine signaling. 1,397,949. November 22, 1921.

Stop-clock. 1,397,950. November 22, 1921.

Method and apparatus for inspecting materials. 1,414,077. April 25, 1922.

Method and apparatus for submarine signaling. 1,415,539. May 9, 1922.

Method and apparatus for detecting, measuring, and utilizing low-frequency impulses. 1,429,497. September 19, 1922.

Acoustic method and apparatus. 1,453,316. May 1, 1923.

Directional receiving of submarine signals. 1,472,558. October 30, 1923.

Eliminating undesired impulses. 1,473,179. November 6, 1923.

Apparatus for producing and receiving signals. 1,486,735. March 11, 1924.

Method and apparatus for signaling. 1,497,366. June 10, 1924.

Submarine signaling. 1,501,105. July 15, 1924.

Eliminating disturbing energy. 1,534,205. April 21, 1925.

Apparatus for amplifying. 1,546,440. July 21, 1925.

Eliminating disturbing noises. 1,547,740. July 28, 1925.

Method and apparatus for generating electrical oscillations. 1,553,152. September 8, 1925.

Apparatus for directive signaling. 1,561,441. November 10, 1925.

Signaling by ultra-audible sound waves. 1,562,950. November 24, 1925.

Channel pilot. 1,574,074. February 23, 1926.

Infusor. 1,576,735. March 16, 1926.

Acoustic method and apparatus. Reissue 16,372. June 29, 1926.

Method and apparatus for coordinating radio and phonograph reproduction. 1,616,416. February 1, 1927.

Book reproducible by radiant energy. 1,616,848. February 8, 1927.

Wireless directive signaling. 1,617,240. February 8, 1927.

Method and apparatus for the transmission of energy by high-frequency impulses. 1,617,241. February 8, 1927.

Wireless transmission and reception. 1,617,242. February 8, 1927.

Method and apparatus for determining distance by echo. 1,636,502. July 19, 1927.

Method and apparatus for producing and reading books. 1,732,302. October 22, 1929.

Method and apparatus for heating buildings. 1,802,970. April 28, 1931.

Method and apparatus for determining distance by echo. 1,853,119. April 12, 1932.

Method and apparatus for generating and detecting impulses. 1,854,025. April 12, 1932.

Apparatus for setting to best photographic exposure.
1,859,621. May 24, 1932.

Loud speaker apparatus and method. 1,863,840. June 21,
1932.

Method and apparatus for coordinating radio and phonograph
reproduction. 1,863,841. June 21, 1932.

Parking cars. 1,882,183. October 11, 1932.

Modulating electrical energy by light impulses. 1,899,026.
February 28, 1933.

Light modulators and constructing the same. 1,901,502.
March 14, 1933.

Rotary brush. 1,901,503. March 14, 1933.

Height indicator. 1,924,032. August 22, 1933.

Method and apparatus for sound transmission. 1,965,226. July
3, 1934.

Height indicator. 1,991,892. February 19, 1935.

Television system. 2,059,221. November 3, 1936. [Issued in
name of Reginald A. Fessenden, deceased, and H. M.
Fessenden, executrix.]

Television apparatus. 2,059,222. November 3, 1936. [Issued
in name of Reginald A. Fessenden, deceased, and H. M.
Fessenden, executrix.]

Title Index

Acoustic method and apparatus. 1,453,316.
Acoustic method and apparatus. Reissue 16,372. June 29, 1926.
Aerial for wireless signaling. 793,651.
Agricultural engineering. 1,121,722.
Amplifying electrical impulses. 1,154,750.
Apparatus and method for producing vibratory motions. 1,207,387.
Apparatus for amplifying. 1,546,440.
Apparatus for converting heat into work. 1,132,465.
Apparatus for directive signaling. 1,348,856; 1,355,598; 1,561,441.
Apparatus for electric signaling. 1,101,914.
Apparatus for generating and receiving electromagnetic waves. 1,158,123.
Apparatus for phonograph-kinetoscopes. 1,213,176.
Apparatus for producing and receiving signals. 1,486,735.
Apparatus for producing high-frequency oscillations. 1,166,892.
Apparatus for setting to best photographic exposure. 1,859,621.
Apparatus for signaling by electromagnetic waves. 706,747.
Apparatus for submarine signaling. 1,348,556.
Apparatus for submarines. 1,291,458.
Apparatus for the transmission and receipt of electrical energy. 1,141,453.
Apparatus for the transmission of energy by electric oscillations. 1,156,677.
Apparatus for transmitting and receiving signals. 777,014.
Apparatus for wireless signaling. 918,307; 1,059,666; 1,165,862.
Apparatus for wireless telegraphy. 706,736; 706,741.
Artificial-leather article. 1,357,449.
Book reproducible by radiant energy. 1,616,848.

Capacity. 793,647; 814,951.

Channel pilot. 1,574,074.

Condenser. 793,777.

Conductor for wireless telegraphy. 706,739.

Contact for electromagnetic mechanism. 1,048,670.

Current-actuated wave-responsive device. 706,744.

Current-operated receiver for electromagnetic waves. 715,043.

Destroying enemy gun positions. 1,383,219; 1,384,030.

Detecting and locating ships. 1,319,145.

Detecting device for wireless telegraphy. 917,574.

Determining frequency of periodic impulses. 1,022,584.

Determining position of vessels. 1,002,141.

Determining positions of vessels. 941,565.

Directional receiving of submarine signals. 1,472,558.

Dynamo-electric machinery. 1,167,366; 1,213,610; 1,213,611.

Electric signaling. 915,280; 962,014; 1,132,568; 1,179,906.

Electric signaling apparatus. 1,050,441.

Electrical apparatus. 962,017.

Electrical signaling. 979,145; 1,002,052.

Electromagnetic indicator. 1,172,018.

Eliminating disturbing energy. 1,534,205.

Eliminating disturbing noises. 1,547,740.

Eliminating undesired impulses. 1,473,179.

Gun-sight. 1,265,766.

Height indicator. 1,924,032; 1,991,892.

High-frequency electrical conductor. 1,039,717.

Incandescent lamp. 638,839; 638,840; 639,161; 650,531; 670,316.

Induction-coil. 654,390.

Induction-coil for X-ray apparatus. 644,972.

Infusor. 1,576,735.

Leading-in wire for incandescent lamps. 452,494.

Light modulators and constructing the same. 1,901,502.

Lightning-arrester. 932,112.

Locating enemy-gun positions. 1,341,795.

Loud speaker apparatus and method. 1,863,840.
Magnetic material. 1,074,424.
Manufacture of incandescent electric lamps. 453,742.
Means for cleaning guns. 938,836.
Means for generating high-frequency electric oscillations. 897,279.
Means for transmission of energy by electromagnetic waves. 1,015,881.
Means of transmitting intelligence. 1,170,969.
Measuring distance. 1,217,585.
Method and apparatus for agricultural engineering. 1,268,949.
Method and apparatus for amplifying electric impulses. 1,196,938.
Method and apparatus for cooling and lubricating systems. 1,331,907.
Method and apparatus for coordinating radio and phonograph reproduction. 1,616,416; 1,863,841.
Method and apparatus for detecting low-frequency impulses. 1,348,825.
Method and apparatus for detecting, measuring, and utilizing low-frequency impulses. 1,429,497.
Method and apparatus for determining distance by echo. 1,636,502; 1,853,119.
Method and apparatus for eliminating undesired vibrations. 1,319,521.
Method and apparatus for generating and detecting impulses. 1,854,025.
Method and apparatus for generating electrical oscillations. 1,553,152.
Method and apparatus for heating buildings. 1,802,970.
Method and apparatus for inspecting materials. 1,414,077.
Method and apparatus for locating ore-bodies. 1,240,328.
Method and apparatus for locating submarines. 1,348,855.
Method and apparatus for producing alternating currents. 1,265,068.

Method and apparatus for producing and reading books.
   1,732,302.
Method and apparatus for signaling. 1,497,366.
Method and apparatus for signaling and otherwise utilizing
   radiant impulses. 1,384,014.
Method and apparatus for sound insulation. 1,348,828.
Method and apparatus for sound transmission. 1,965,226.
Method and apparatus for submarine signaling. 1,207,388;
   1,348,827; 1,394,483; 1,397,949; 1,415,539.
Method and apparatus for submarine signaling and detection.
   1,348,826.
Method and apparatus for the transmission of energy by high-
   frequency impulses. 1,617,241.
Method and apparatus for transmitting and receiving sound-
   waves through ground. 1,270,398.
Method of and apparatus for heat insulation. 1,301,675.
Method of and apparatus for obtaining increased circulation.
   1,318,740.
Method of and apparatus for reproducing impulses. 1,133,435.
Method of signaling. 962,018.
Modulating electrical energy by light impulses. 1,899,026.
Molding for electrical conductors. 506,311.
Multiplex telegraphy. 981,406.
Parking cars. 1,882,183.
Pencil for incandescent lamps. 638,837; 638,838.
Power plant. 1,217,165.
Power generation. 1,214,531.
Producing high-frequency oscillations. 932,111; 1,166,893.
Receiver for electric signaling. 962,015.
Receiver for electromagnetic waves. 727,327; 727,331;
   793,648; 916,429; 921,531; 962,016; 1,022,539;
   1,042,778.
Receiver for electromagnetic waves. Reissue 12,115. May 26,
   1903.
Receiver for signaling. 727,328; 1,002,050.
Receiving electromagnetic waves. 1,044,637.

Rotary brush. 1,901,503.
Selective signaling. 752,894.
Selective signaling by electromagnetic waves. 715,203;
    727,326.
Sending mechanism for electromagnetic waves. 1,126,966.
Signaling. 916,428; 1,019,236; 1,050,728; 1,182,843.
Signaling apparatus for aerial navigation. 1,158,124.
Signaling by electromagnetic waves. 706,745; 706,746;
    727,329; 727,330; 730,753; 742,779; 742,780; 752,895;
    753,864; 754,058; 793,649; 793,650; 793,652; 956,489;
    998,567; 1,002,049; 1,002,051; 1,020,032; 1,080,271;
    1,182,003; 1,184,843.
Signaling by sound and other longitudinal elastic impulses.
    1,108,895.
Signaling by ultra-audible sound waves. 1,562,950.
Sound-producer. 1,277,562.
Sound signaling. 1,384,029.
Stop-clock. 1,397,950.
Storage and care of wheeled vehicles. 1,114,975.
Submarine signaling. 1,311,157; 1,318,739; 1,394,482;
    1,501,105.
Submarine, subterranean, and aerial telephony. 1,212,202.
System of storing power. 1,112,441; 1,247,520.
Television apparatus. 2,059,222.
Television system. 2,059,221.
Transmission and receipt of electrical energy. 979,144.
Transmission and receipt of signals. 740,261.
Transmitting and receiving electrical energy. 1,141,386.
Transmitting and receiving signals. 1,157,094.
Transmitting energy by electromagnetic waves. 1,172,017.
Utilizing pulverulent matter as fuel. 1,191,072.
Utilizing the energy of waves. 731,029.
Wheel-puller. 1,357,698.
Wireless direction-finder. 1,374,293.
Wireless directive signaling. 1,617,240.

Wireless signaling. 706,740; 706,742; 706,743; 753,863;
    918,306; 960,631; 1,022,540; 1,074,423; 1,101,915;
    1,176,282; 1,178,507.
Wireless telegraphy. 706,735; 706,737; 706,738, 793,718;
    897,278; 923,962; 923,963; 948,068; 974,762;
    1,035,334; 1,045,781; 1,045,782; 1,059,665; 1,132,569;
    1,147,010; 1,175,418.
Wireless telegraphy. Reissue 12,168. November 10, 1903.
Wireless telegraphy. Reissue 12,169. November 10, 1903.
Wireless transmission and reception. 1,617,242.
X-ray apparatus. 648,660.

JOHN A. FLEMING (1849-1945)

Preparation of materials for use in electric insulation. 259,271. June 6, 1882. 21:1777.

Preparation or production of insulating materials or articles. 284,289. September 4, 1883. 24:931.

Preparation and production of insulating materials or articles. 319,084. June 2, 1885. 31:1083.

Electric-arc lamp. 653,572. July 10, 1900. 92:331.

Device for wireless telegraphy. 758,004. April 19, 1904. 109:2140.

Apparatus employed in wireless telegraphy. 758,005. April 19, 1904. 109:2141.

Transmitter apparatus for wireless telegraphy. 792,014. June 13, 1905. 116:1747.

Telegraphic signaling-key. 792,015. June 13, 1905. 116:1748.

Instrument for converting alternating electric currents into continuous currents. 803,684. November 7, 1905. 119:72.

Apparatus for measuring the length of electric waves. 804,189. November 7, 1905. 119:293.

Instrument for making electrical measurements. 804,190.
November 7, 1905. 119:294.

Instrument for detecting electric oscillations. 954,619. April
12, 1910. 153:349.

Thermionic device. 1,486,237. March 11, 1924.

Title Index

Apparatus employed in wireless telegraphy. 758,005.
Apparatus for measuring the length of electric waves.
    804,189.
Device for wireless telegraphy. 758,004.
Diode. *See* 954,619.
Electric-arc lamp. 653,572.
Instrument for converting alternating electric currents into
    continuous currents. 803,684.
Instrument for detecting electric oscillations. 954,619.
Instrument for making electrical measurements. 804,190.
Preparation and production of insulating materials or articles.
    319,084.
Preparation of materials for use in electric insulation. 259,271.
Preparation or production of insulating materials or articles.
    284,289.
Telegraphic signaling-key. 792,015.
Thermionic device. 1,486,237.
Transmitter apparatus for wireless telegraphy. 792,014.
Vacuum tube diode. *See* 954,619.

HUGO GERNSBACK (1884-1967)

Battery-cell. 842,950. February 5, 1907. 126:1843.

Incandescent lamp. 902,069. October 27, 1908. 136:1819.

Electrorheostat-regulator. 948,275. February 1, 1910. 151:166.

Electro-adjustable condenser. 951,788. March 8, 1910. 152:464.

Detectorium. 961,855. June 21, 1910. 155:596.

Relay. 978,999. December 20, 1910. 161:600.

Potentiometer. 988,456. April 4, 1911. 165:57.

Electrolytic interrupter. 988,767. April 4, 1911. 165:164.

Combined electric hair brush and comb. 1,016,138. January 30, 1912. 174:1161.

Rotary variable condenser. 1,033,095. July 23, 1912. 180:894.

Luminous electric mirror. 1,057,820. April 1, 1913. 189:146.

Transmitter. 1,124,413. January 12, 1915. 210:466.

Postal card. 1,209,425. December 19, 1916. 233:1003.

Telephone-headband. 1,329,658. February 3, 1920. 271:58.

Electromagnetic sending device. 1,354,389. September 28, 1920. 278:667.

Submersible amusement device. 1,384,750. July 19, 1921. 288:440.

Apparatus for landing flying-machines. 1,392,140. September 27, 1921. 290:748.

Tuned telephone receiver. 1,478,709. December 25, 1923.

Electric valve. 1,488,337. March 25, 1924.

Detector. 1,496,671. June 3, 1924.

Ear cushion. 1,514,152. November 4, 1924.

Acoustic apparatus. 1,521,287. December 30, 1924.

Radiocabinet. Design 67,451. June 2, 1925.

Radiocabinet. Design 67,452. June 2, 1925.

Cord terminal. 1,557,248. October 13, 1925.

Coil mounting. 1,558,604. October 27, 1925.

Radiohorn. 1,560,684. November 10, 1925.

Variable condenser. 1,562,629. November 24, 1925.

Electrical switch. 1,585,485. May 18, 1926.

Telephone receiver. 1,587,719. June 8, 1926.

Crystal detector. 1,590,236. June 29, 1926.

Mounting inductances. 1,618,002. February 15, 1927.

Depilator. 1,620,539. March 8, 1927.

Switch. 1,695,957. December 18, 1928.

Code learner's instrument. 1,801,734. April 21, 1931.

Electrically operated fountain. 1,954,704. April 10, 1934.
[With Joseph H. Kraus and S. Gernsback.]

Hydraulic fishery. 2,718,083. September 20, 1955.

Title Index

Acoustic apparatus. 1,521,287.
Apparatus for landing flying-machines. 1,392,140.
Battery-cell. 842,950.
Code learner's instrument. 1,801,734.
Coil mounting. 1,558,604.
Combined electric hair brush and comb. 1,016,138.
Cord terminal. 1,557,248.
Crystal detector. 1,590,236.
Depilator. 1,620,539.
Detector. 1,496,671.
Detectorium. 961,855.
Ear cushion. 1,514,152.
Electric valve. 1,488,337.
Electrical switch. 1,585,485.
Electrically operated fountain. 1,954,704.
Electro-adjustable condenser. 951,788.
Electrolytic interrupter. 988,767.
Electromagnetic sending device. 1,354,389.

Electrorheostat-regulator. 948,275.
Hydraulic fishery. 2,718,083.
Incandescent lamp. 902,069.
Luminous electric mirror. 1,057,820.
Mounting inductances. 1,618,002.
Postal card. 1,209,425.
Potentiometer. 988,456.
Radiocabinet. Design 67,451; 67,452. June 2, 1925.
Radiohorn. 1,560,684.
Relay. 978,999.
Rotary variable condenser. 1,033,095.
Submersible amusement device. 1,384,750.
Switch. 1,695,957.
Telephone-headband. 1,329,658.
Telephone receiver. 1,587,719.
Transmitter. 1,124,413.
Tuned telephone receiver. 1,478,709.
Variable condenser. 1,562,629.

ALFRED N. GOLDSMITH (1888-1974)

Wireless signaling system. 1,323,759. December 2, 1919.
269:100.

System for producing oscillations. 1,334,087. March 16,
1920. 272:474.

Radiosignaling system. 1,347,328. July 20, 1920. 276:516.

Radio receiving system. 1,396,571. November 8, 1921. [With
J. Weinberger.]

Signaling system. 1,404,756. January 31, 1922.

Method and apparatus for receiving sustained wave signals.
1,432,455. October 17, 1922.

Method and apparatus for receiving sustained wave signals.
1,432,456. October 17, 1922.

Variable electrical controlling element. 1,564,555. December
8, 1925.

Apparatus for wave changing in radiosignaling. 1,571,405.
February 2, 1926.

Radiotelephony. 1,622,033. March 22, 1927. [With J.
Weinberger.]

Antenna. 1,683,773. September 11, 1928.

Sound-reproducing machine. 1,702,770. February 19, 1929.

Radio receiving apparatus. 1,708,539. April 9, 1929.

Electrical signaling system and signaling method. 1,712,036. May 7, 1929. [With A. F. Van Dyck.]

Radio receiving system. 1,717,201. June 11, 1929.

Sound-reproducing machine. 1,721,151. July 16, 1929.

Combined radioreceiver and phonograph reproducer and recorder. 1,724,191. August 13, 1929.

Combined electric phonograph recorder and reproducer. 1,735,113. November 12, 1929.

Combined radio and phonograph cabinet. 1,757,304. May 6, 1930.

Reproducer arm. 1,760,306. May 27, 1930.

Radio signaling system. 1,761,118. June 3, 1930.

Television system. 1,770,205. July 8, 1930. [With J. Weinberger.]

Automatic switching device for electric phonographs. 1,816,577. July 28, 1931.

Statistical directional transmitter. 1,821,383. September 1, 1931.

Sound reproducing machine. 1,876,913. September 13, 1932.

Sound reproducer. 1,902,442. March 21, 1933. [With I. Wolff.]

Ultra-short wave repeating system. 1,918,262. July 18, 1933.

Television system. 1,924,277. August 29, 1933.

Signal relaying system. 1,927,827. September 26, 1933.

Sound motion picture. 1,946,206. February 6, 1934.

Home talking movie combination. 1,971,446. August 28, 1934.

Talking motion picture apparatus. 2,000,697. May 7, 1935.

Radio receiving system. 2,004,107. June 11, 1935.

Motion picture. 2,032,410. March 3, 1936.

Television system. 2,043,997. June 16, 1936.

Radio receiving set. 2,068,233. January 19, 1937.

Television system. 2,073,370. March 9, 1937. [With T. R. Goldsborough.]

Over-modulation protective device. 2,079,446. May 4, 1937.

Public address system and the like. 2,081,625. May 25, 1937.

Synthetic reverberation system. 2,105,318. January 11, 1938.

Phonographic apparatus. 2,113,401. April 5, 1938.

System for the reproduction of sound. 2,114,680. April 19, 1938.

Phonograph with automatically compensated tone and volume control. 2,118,602. May 24, 1938.

Control system. 2,134,757. November 1, 1938.

Automobile radio and communication system. 2,138,598. November 29, 1938.

Radio relay and distribution system. 2,155,821. April 25, 1939.

Automatic volume control. 2,167,058. July 25, 1939. [With A. F. Van Dyck.]

Television system. 2,168,566. August 8, 1939.

Television control system. 2,172,936. September 12, 1939.

Motion picture apparatus for approach shots. 2,178,228. October 31, 1939.

Signaling system. 2,181,564. November 28, 1939.

Production of still or motion pictures. 2,183,217. December 12, 1939.

Television control. 2,193,869. March 19, 1940.

Nested remote and local control units. 2,199,371. April 30, 1940.

Recording and reproducing of sound. 2,207,249. July 9, 1940.

Production of sound picture records. 2,211,416. August 13, 1940.

Television system. 2,219,149. October 22, 1940.

Television system. 2,221,091. November 12, 1940.

Television scanning device. 2,227,080. December 31, 1940.

Television-telephone system. 2,236,501. April 1, 1941.

Composite-delineation television. 2,236,502. April 1, 1941.

Television control device. 2,244,251. June 3, 1941.

Image formation. 2,244,687. June 10, 1941. [With H. R. Menefee, W. Mayer, and F. Kastilan.]

Image formation and apparatus for forming images. 2,244,688. June 10, 1941. [With H. R. Menefee, W. Mayer, and F. Kastilan.]

Relay system monitoring. 2,250,950. July 29, 1941.

Color television system. 2,253,292. August 19, 1941.

Color television system. 2,259,884. October 21, 1941.

Microfacsimile system. 2,275,898. March 10, 1942.

Thermal optical image reproducing system. 2,280,946. April 28, 1942.

Multiplex signaling system. 2,282,046. May 5, 1942.

Televisible guiding system. 2,298,476. October 13, 1942.

Multiple frequency modulation system. 2,301,395. November 10, 1942.

Electronic system. 2,302,311. November 17, 1942.

Modulation system. 2,304,163. December 8, 1942.

Television system. 2,307,210. January 5, 1943.

Television image enlarging system. 2,307,211. January 5, 1943.

Picture centering control apparatus. 2,307,212. January 5, 1943.

Television transmitter. 2,322,355. June 22, 1943.

Television system. 2,335,180. November 23, 1943.

Electrical energy generating system. 2,338,239. January 4, 1944.

Television studio lighting. 2,343,971. March 14, 1944.

Television transmitting system. 2,344,695. March 21, 1944.

Remote control system. 2,345,472. March 28, 1944.

Automatic reverberation control. 2,354,176. July 18, 1944.

Television apparatus. 2,354,591. July 25, 1944.

Television system. 2,359,637. October 3, 1944.

Wave control circuit. 2,367,116. January 9, 1945.

Television transmitting system. 2,381,901. August 14, 1945.

Television transmitting system. 2,381,902. August 14, 1945.

Television apparatus. 2,384,260. September 4, 1945.

Color television system. 2,389,039. November 13, 1945.

Television system. 2,398,705. April 16, 1946.

Impulse counting and selecting device. 2,401,729. June 11, 1946.

Secret communication system. 2,405,252. August 6, 1946.

Statistical system. 2,413,965. January 7, 1947.

Color television system. 2,416,918. March 4, 1947.

Television apparatus. 2,416,919. March 4, 1947.

Color television system. 2,423,769. July 8, 1947.

Color television system. 2,423,770. July 8, 1947.

Radio centercasting system. 2,427,670. September 23, 1947.

Color television system. 2,431,115. November 18, 1947.

Centercasting network system. 2,465,976. March 29, 1949.

Radio guiding system. 2,481,410. September 6, 1949.

Color television. 2,481,839. September 13, 1949.

Radio centercasting selection apparatus. 2,488,508. November 15, 1949.

Television system. 2,509,038. May 23, 1950.

Color television apparatus. 2,516,314. July 25, 1950.

Color television system. 2,531,508. November 28, 1950.

Color facsimile scanning device. 2,548,783. April 10, 1951.

Signal transmission system. 2,557,278. June 19, 1951.

Color television system. 2,560,168. July 10, 1951.

Television inspection system. 2,561,197. July 17, 1951.

Stereoscopic and stereosonic television system. 2,566,700. September 4, 1951.

Cabinet for television receivers. 2,566,830. September 4, 1951.

Automatic registration of component color images. 2,568,543. September 18, 1951.

Stereoscopic television system. 2,578,298. December 11, 1951.

Sensitizing, recording and desensitizing apparatus. 2,602,016. July 1, 1952.

Electrical recording in colors. 2,609,440. September 2, 1952.

Composite picture television. 2,610,242. September 9, 1952.

Color phasing system. 2,627,548. February 3, 1953.

Multicolor television. 2,630,542. March 3, 1953.

Television secrecy system. 2,636,936. April 28, 1953.

Subtractive color television. 2,645,976. July 21, 1953.

Inspection system. 2,648,723. August 11, 1953.

Additive color television. 2,653,183. September 22, 1953.

Color micro-facsimile system. 2,658,102. November 3, 1953.

Production of multilinear screens. 2,669,768. February 23, 1954.

Color television system. 2,686,218. August 10, 1954.

Television scanning system. 2,703,339. March 1, 1955.

Color television and pick-up tubes. 2,728,011. December 20, 1955.

Air conditioning system. 2,835,186. May 20, 1958.

Projector cooling system. 2,837,965. June 10, 1958.

Television systems. 2,989,580. June 20, 1961. [With R. C. Kennedy.]

Three dimensional television system. 3,674,921. July 4, 1972.

Title Index

Image formation. 2,244,687.

Image formation and apparatus for forming images.
2,244,688.

Impulse counting and selecting device. 2,401,729.

Inspection system. 2,648,723.

Method and apparatus for receiving sustained wave signals.
1,432,455; 1,432,456.

Microfacsimile system. 2,275,898.

Modulation system. 2,304,163.

Motion picture. 2,032,410.

Motion picture apparatus for approach shots. 2,178,228.

Multicolor television. 2,630,542.

Multiple frequency modulation system. 2,301,395.

Multiplex signaling system. 2,282,046.

Nested remote and local control units. 2,199,371.

Over-modulation protective device. 2,079,446.

Phonograph with automatically compensated tone and volume
control. 2,118,602.

Phonographic apparatus. 2,113,401.

Picture centering control apparatus. 2,307,212.

Production of multilinear screens. 2,669,768.

Production of sound picture records. 2,211,416.

Production of still or motion pictures. 2,183,217.

Projector cooling system. 2,837,965.

Public address system and the like. 2,081,625.

Radio centercasting selection apparatus. 2,488,508.

Radio centercasting system. 2,427,670.

Radio guiding system. 2,481,410.

Radio receiving apparatus. 1,708,539.

Radio receiving set. 2,068,233.

Radio receiving system. 1,396,571; 1,717,201; 2,004,107.

Radio relay and distribution system. 2,155,821.

Radio signaling system. 1,761,118.

Radiosignaling system. 1,347,328.

Radiotelephony. 1,622,033.

Recording and reproducing of sound. 2,207,249.

Relay system monitoring. 2,250,950.
Remote control system. 2,345,472.
Reproducer arm. 1,760,306.
Secret communication system. 2,405,252.
Sensitizing, recording and desensitizing apparatus. 2,602,016.
Signal relaying system. 1,927,827.
Signal transmission system. 2,557,278.
Signaling system. 1,404,756; 2,181,564.
Sound motion picture. 1,946,206.
Sound reproducer. 1,902,442.
Sound reproducing machine. 1,702,770; 1,721,151; 1,876,913.
Statistical directional transmitter. 1,821,383.
Statistical system. 2,413,965.
Stereoscopic and stereosonic television system. 2,566,700.
Stereoscopic television system. 2,578,298.
Subtractive color television. 2,645,976.
Synthetic reverberation system. 2,105,318.
System for producing oscillations. 1,334,087.
System for the reproduction of sound. 2,114,680.
Talking motion picture apparatus. 2,000,697.
Televisible guiding system. 2,298,476.
Television apparatus. 2,354,591; 2,384,260; 2,416,919.
Television control. 2,193,869.
Television control device. 2,244,251.
Television control system. 2,172,936.
Television image enlarging system. 2,307,211.
Television inspection system. 2,561,197.
Television scanning device. 2,227,080.
Television scanning system. 2,703,339.
Television secrecy system. 2,636,936.
Television studio lighting. 2,343,971.
Television system. 1,770,205; 1,924,277; 2,043,997; 2,073,370; 2,168,566; 2,219,149; 2,221,091; 2,307,210; 2,335,180; 2,359,637; 2,398,705; 2,509,038.
Television systems. 2,989,580.

Television-telephone system. 2,236,501.
Television transmitter. 2,322,355.
Television transmitting system. 2,344,695; 2,381,901;
    2,381,902.
Thermal optical image reproducing system. 2,280,946.
Three dimensional television system. 3,674,921.
Ultra-short wave repeating system. 1,918,262.
Variable electrical controlling element. 1,564,555.
Wave control circuit. 2,367,116.
Wireless signaling system. 1,323,759.

LOUIS HAZELTINE (1886-1964)

[Note: Patents assigned to the Hazeltine Corporation or Hazeltine Research, Inc., but not in Hazeltine's name are not listed.]

Shielding radio apparatus. 1,379,184. May 24, 1921. 286:717

Method and electric-circuit arrangement for neutralizing capacity coupling. 1,450,080. March 27, 1923.

Method and means for neutralizing capacity coupling in audions. 1,489,228. April 1, 1924.

Neutralizing capacity coupling in audions. 1,533,858. April 14, 1925.

Eliminating magnetic coupling between coils. 1,577,421. March 16, 1926.

Wave signaling system. 1,648,808. November 8, 1927.

Wave signaling system. 1,649,589. November 15, 1927.

Wave signaling system. 1,650,353. November 22, 1927.

Signaling system. 1,656,888. January 17, 1928.

Method and apparatus for converting electric power. 1,657,574. January 31, 1928.

Wave signaling system. 1,658,638. February 7, 1928.

Wave signaling system. 1,692,257. November 20, 1928.

System of radiocommunication. 1,697,650. January 1, 1929.

Eliminating magnetic coupling. 1,698,364. January 8, 1929.

Method and apparatus for converting electric power.
1,702,402. February 19, 1929.

Wave signaling system. Reissue 17,530. December 17, 1929.

Unicontrol signaling system. 1,755,114. April 15, 1930.

Variable condenser. 1,755,115. April 15, 1930.

Method and apparatus for converting electric power.
1,803,184. April 28, 1931.

Method and apparatus for converting direct current into
alternating current by electrostatically controlled oscillations.
1,835,156. December 8, 1931.

Antenna coupling system. 1,852,710. April 5, 1932.

Radio receiving system. 1,869,804. August 2, 1932.

Method and apparatus for converting electric power.
1,904,455. April 18, 1933.

Frequency conversion system. 2,113,464. April 5, 1938.

Frequency conversion system. Reissue 21,153. July 18, 1939.

Electron discharge device. 2,172,750. September 12, 1939.

Title Index

Antenna coupling system. 1,852,710.

Electron discharge device. 2,172,750.

Eliminating magnetic coupling. 1,698,364.

Eliminating magnetic coupling between coils. 1,577,421.

Frequency conversion system. 2,113,464.

Frequency conversion system. Reissue 21,153. July 18, 1939.

Method and apparatus for converting direct current into alternating current by electrostatically controlled oscillations. 1,835,156.

Method and apparatus for converting electric power. 1,657,574; 1,702,402; 1,803,184; 1,904,455.

Method and electric-circuit arrangement for neutralizing capacity coupling. 1,450,080.

Method and means for neutralizing capacity coupling in audions. 1,489,228.

Neutralizing capacity coupling in audions. 1,533,858.

Neutrodyne circuit. *See* 1,533,858.

Radio receiving system. 1,869,804.

Shielding radio apparatus. 1,379,184.

Signaling system. 1,656,888.

System of radiocommunication. 1,697,650.

Unicontrol signaling system. 1,755,114.

Variable condenser. 1,755,115.

Wave signaling system. 1,648,808; 1,649,589; 1,650,353; 1,658,638; 1,692,257.

Wave signaling system. Reissue 17,530. December 17, 1929.

JOHN V. L. HOGAN (1890-1960)

Detector for wireless communication. 950,781. March 1, 1910. 152:110.

Apparatus for wireless signaling. 1,014,002. January 9, 1912. 174:345.

Break-key. 1,016,564. February 6, 1912. 175:114.

Transmitting intelligence by radiant energy. 1,141,717. June 1, 1915. 215:223. [With John W. Lee, S. M. Kintner, and H. M. Barrett.]

Oscillating-current meter. 1,152,632. September 7, 1915. 218:93. [With S. M. Kintner and H. M. Barrett.]

Radiosignaling. 1,350,100. August 17, 1920. 277:508.

Receiver for wireless telegraphy. 1,363,319. December 28, 1920. 281:600. [With S. M. Kintner and H. M. Barrett.]

Demountable rim. 1,389,345. August 30, 1921. 289:906. [With Thomas E. Dunbar and H. Crevasse.]

Arc transmission system. 1,537,609. May 12, 1925.

Acoustic device. 1,776,223. September 16, 1930.

Television method and apparatus. 1,943,238. January 9, 1934. [With H. P. Donle.]

Television transmission. 1,976,699. October 9, 1934.

Television scanning system. 1,994,708. March 19, 1935.

Television synchronization. 1,998,812. April 23, 1935.

Scanning system. 2,010,764. August 8, 1935.

System for television and sound. 2,049,384. July 28, 1936.

Recording paper system. 2,111,776. March 22, 1938.

Facsimile system. 2,149,292. March 7, 1939. [With H. G. Miller.]

Means and method for facsimile recording. 2,173,113. September 19, 1939. [With H. G. Miller.]

Facsimile recorder. 2,202,855. June 4, 1940. [With H. C. Ressler.]

Cathode ray system. 2,212,640. August 27, 1940.

Facsimile apparatus. 2,239,489. April 22, 1941. [With H. G. Miller.]

Electrolytic recording. 2,339,267. January 18, 1944. [With H. C. Ressler.]

Facsimile scanner drum. 2,356,999. August 29, 1944.

Registering radio listening habits. 2,368,761. February 6, 1945.

Facsimile apparatus. 2,379,438. July 3, 1945.

Continuous facsimile scanner. 2,379,906. July 10, 1945.

Graphic privacy system. 2,414,101. January 14, 1947. [With H. C. Ressler.]

Graphic privacy system. 2,437,255. March 9, 1948. [With H. C. Ressler.]

Facsimile recorder construction. 2,575,959. November 20, 1951.

Quantity recorder. 2,587,319. February 26, 1952.

Title Index

Recording paper system. 2,111,776.
Registering radio listening habits. 2,368,761.
Scanning system. 2,010,764.
Single dial tuning. *See* 1,014,002.
System for television and sound. 2,049,384.
Television method and apparatus. 1,943,238.
Television scanning system. 1,994,708.
Television synchronization. 1,998,812.
Television transmission. 1,976,699.
Transmitting intelligence by radiant energy. 1,141,717.

HARRY HOUCK (1896-1989)

Method and apparatus for selectively transferring electrical oscillatory energy. 1,438,828. December 12, 1922.

Radiofrequency transformer. 1,599,531. September 14, 1926.

Arrangement of electrical appliances. 1,684,703. September 18, 1928.

Wave signaling system. 1,686,005. October 2, 1928.

Adjustable electrical condenser. 1,715,319. May 28, 1929.

Variable tuning inductance device. 1,719,161. July 2, 1929. [With W. Aull, Jr.]

Loud-speaker motor. 1,788,557. January 13, 1931. [With W. Aull, Jr.]

Electron-tube apparatus. 1,797,205. March 17, 1931.

Condenser testing equipment. 1,823,492. September 15, 1931.

Electrical filter. 1,824,819. September 29, 1931.

Rectifier. 1,829,897. November 3, 1931.

Filter system. 1,833,867. November 24, 1931.

Filtering arrangement for direct current. 1,840,776. January 12, 1932.

Thermionic valve. 1,905,872. April 25, 1933.

Condenser. 1,934,192. November 7, 1933.

Amplifying apparatus. 2,054,421. September 15, 1936.

Trimmer condenser. 2,150,973. March 21, 1939.

Resistance element. 2,330,783. July 28, 1943. [With O. J. Morelock.]

Selective transfer of electrical oscillatory energy. 2,336,498. December 14, 1943. [With J. B. Minter 2nd.]

Multistage frequency measurement system utilizing predetermined frequency slip factors. 3,102,980. September 3, 1963.

Title Index

Multistage frequency measurement system utilizing
   predetermined frequency slip factors. 3,102,980.
Radiofrequency transformer. 1,599,531.
Rectifier. 1,829,897.
Resistance element. 2,330,783.
Selective transfer of electrical oscillatory energy. 2,336,498.
Thermionic valve. 1,905,872.
Trimmer condenser. 2,150,973.
Variable tuning inductance device. 1,719,161.
Wave signaling system. 1,686,005.

CHARLES F. JENKINS (1867-1934)

[Note: Patents assigned to the Jenkins Television Corporation but not in Jenkins' name are not listed.]

Phantoscope. 536,569. March 26, 1895. 70:1776.

Kinetographic camera. 560,800. May 26, 1896. 75:1261.

Phantoscope. 586,953. July 20, 1897. 80:501. [With T. Armat.]

Device for obtaining stereoscopic effects in exhibiting pictures. 606,993. July 5, 1898. 84:122.

Photographic-printing apparatus. 649,730. May 15, 1900. 91:1367.

Stereoscopic mutoscope. 671,111. April 2, 1901. 95:72.

Hydrocarbon-burner. 711,925. October 21, 1902. 101:647.

Vapor-burner. 731,370. June 16, 1903. 104:1859.

Moving-picture apparatus. 779,364. January 3, 1905. 114:229.

Bag-closure. 805,205. November 21, 1905. 119:827.

Automatic sign-changing letter. 808,884. January 2, 1906. 120:117. [With E. C. Thomas.]

Heating apparatus. 817,173. April 10, 1906. 121:1693.

Automobile steering device. 818,967. April 24, 1906. 121:2575.

Motion-picture machine. 819,514. May 1, 1906. 122:212. [With J. E. Cahill.]

Bottle-filling machine. 828,117. August 7, 1906. 123:1882.

Paper receptacle. 838,416. December 11, 1906. 125:1965.

Making paper-tube caps. 860,385. July 16, 1907. 129:1115.

Motion-picture apparatus. 865,593. September 10, 1907. 130:426.

Receptacle for materials to be applied with a brush. 891,262. June 23, 1908. 134:1822.

Telautograph. 909,421. January 12, 1909. 138:356.

Making spirally-wound tubes. 916,162. March 23, 1909. 140:904.

Cap for bottles. 919,872. April 27, 1909. 141:1067.

Liquid-holding paper vessel. 920,150. May 4, 1909. 142:18.

Apparatus for making spirally-wound tubes. 921,842. May 18, 1909. 142:638.

Making paper bottle-closures. 924,555. June 8, 1909.
143:512.

Paper package. 925,913. June 22, 1909. 143:1024.

Steam-generator flue. 926,700. June 29, 1909. 143:1319.

Steam-generator flue. 926,701. June 29, 1909. 143:1319.

Machine for making paper bottles. 933,460. September 7,
1909. 146:146.

Motion-picture camera. 934,894. September 21, 1909.
146:669. [With O. B. Depue.]

Paper vessel. 935,029. September 28, 1909. 146:740.

Die for making closures for paper bottles. 935,791. October
5, 1909. 147:58.

Treating paper bottles. 935,848. October 5, 1909. 147:76.

Ball-bearing. 937,811. October 26, 1909. 147:799.

Apparatus for making spirally-wound tubes. 941,255.
November 23, 1909. 148:1039.

Folding box. 941,256. November 23, 1909. 148:1040.

Folding box. 941,257. November 23, 1909. 148:1040.

Paper receptacle. 941,992. November 30, 1909. 148:1307.

Electrical contact device. 942,647. December 7, 1909.
149:210.

Closure for paper packages. 943,307. December 14, 1909. 149:463.

Paper receptacle. 944,613. December 28, 1909. 149:968.

Knockdown box. 944,614. December 28, 1909. 149:968.

Closure for paper vessels. 944,615. December 28, 1909. 149:968.

Package for frangible articles. 944,616. December 28, 1909. 149:969.

Collapsible knockdown box. 947,179. January 18, 1910. 150:789.

Key and lock. 947,913. February 1, 1910. 151:47.

Paper bottle. 949,036. February 15, 1910. 151:474.

Package for chemicals. 949,708. February 15, 1910. 151:696.

Apparatus for making and inserting bottle-caps. 950,022. February 22, 1910. 151:843.

Spirally-wound collapsible receptacle. 952,258. March 15, 1910. 152:651.

Paper receptacle. 954,104. April 5, 1910. 153:148.

Paper receptacle. 954,105. April 5, 1910. 153:148.

Machine for inserting closures in receptacles. 954,106. April 5, 1910. 153:148.

Apparatus for forming and inserting receptacle-closures. 954,107. April 5, 1910. 153:149.

Apparatus for securing closures in paper tubes. 954,108. April 5, 1910. 153:149.

Bottle-closing device. 954,109. April 5, 1910. 153:149.

Machine for forming and cutting off tubes. 957,966. May 17, 1910. 154:560.

Device for holding bottle-bodies for the insertion of closures. 958,252. May 17, 1910. 154:660.

Apparatus for making paper bottles. 960,226. May 31, 1910. 154:1382.

Machine for making tubes. 964,162. July 12, 1910. 156:408.

Closure for receptacles. 970,926. September 20, 1910. 158:651.

Explosion-motor. 972,379. October 11, 1910. 159:328.

Explosion-engine. 972,380. October 11, 1910. 159:328.

Paper-box machinery. 972,767. October 11, 1910. 159:463.

Mailing-folder. 974,276. November 1, 1910. 160:66.

Bottle-capping machine. 979,766. December 27, 1910. 161:885.

Knockdown box. 981,277. January 10, 1911. 162:412.

Tube-winding device. 982,430. January 24, 1911. 162:861.

Receptacle-labeling apparatus. 983,060. January 31, 1911. 162:1102.

Warning-signal. 983,236. January 31, 1911. 162:1161.

Paper-tube machinery. 984,002. February 14, 1911. 163:284.

Machine for inserting closures in receptacles. 985,900. March 7, 1911. 164:49.

Coating paper receptacles. 985,901. March 7, 1911. 164:50.

Glue-applying apparatus for box-machines. 985,902. March 7, 1911. 164:50.

Making receptacle-closures. 988,716. April 4, 1911. 165:147.

Making boxes or bottles. 991,509. May 9, 1911. 166:273.

Closure for paper vessels. 993,170. May 23, 1911. 166:906.

Two-cycle gas-engine. 997,195. July 4, 1911. 168:204.

Starting device for gas-engines. 1,003,750. September 19, 1911. 170:609.

Railway-tie. 1,003,751. September 19, 1911. 170:609.

Gas-motor starter. 1,003,752. September 19, 1911. 170:609.

Blast-furnace. 1,010,265. November 28, 1911. 172:1024.

Acetylene generating and storing apparatus. 1,010,266. November 28, 1911. 172:1025.

Motion-picture apparatus. 1,010,370. November 28, 1911.
172:1059.

Closure-making machine. 1,017,549. February 13, 1912.
175:489.

Tapering metal bodies. 1,017,671. February 20, 1912.
175:566.

Motion-picture apparatus. 1,017,672. February 20, 1912.
175:566.

Starting device for internal-combustion engines. 1,024,077.
April 4, 1912. 177:875.

Tire-repair device. 1,024,078. April 23, 1912. 177:876.

Wheel-rim. 1,032,286. July 9, 1912. 180:538.

Picture-film rack. 1,045,410. November 26, 1912. 184:912.

Gas-engine starter. 1,047,527. December 17, 1912. 185:672.

Motion-picture apparatus. 1,047,528. December 17, 1912.
185:673.

Valve. 1,047,529. December 17, 1912. 185:673.

Apparatus for providing boxes with closures. 1,047,530.
December 17, 1912. 185:673.

Valve. 1,047,531. December 17, 1912. 185:673.

Apparatus for making paper tubes. 1,047,946. December 24,
1912. 185:846.

Vehicle-tire. 1,062,011. May 20, 1913. 190:570.

Adhesive-applying device. 1,064,738. June 17, 1913. 191:607.

Box-capping machine. 1,067,431. July 15, 1913. 192:593.

Flying-machine. 1,067,432. July 15, 1913. 192:593.

Flying-machine. 1,081,504. December 16, 1913. 197:612.

Moving-picture apparatus. 1,083,016. December 30, 1913. 197:1190.

Flying-machine. 1,085,263. January 27, 1914. 198:767.

Aeroplane-engine. 1,089,645. March 10, 1914. 200:381.

Motion-picture camera. 1,089,646. March 10, 1914. 200:381.

Picture-projecting device. 1,090,622. March 17, 1914. 200:762.

Motion-picture apparatus. 1,091,343. March 24, 1914. 200:1034.

Aeroplane or flying-machine. 1,092,365. April 7, 1914. 201:83.

Film-winding device. 1,093,933. April 21, 1914. 201:691.

Internal-combustion engine. 1,098,805. June 2, 1914. 203:152.

Coating with fusible material. 1,139,291. May 11, 1915. 214:588.

Motion-picture apparatus. 1,152,515. September 7, 1915. 218:49.

View-changing device. 1,153,110. September 7, 1915. 218:262.

Picture-projecting apparatus. 1,153,163. September 7, 1915. 218:281.

Motion-picture apparatus. 1,153,164. September 7, 1915. 218:281.

Device for underwater exploration. 1,156,782. October 12, 1915. 219:532.

Motion-picture apparatus. 1,163,757. December 14, 1915. 221:404.

Device for aerial warfare. 1,173,522. February 29, 1916. 223:1511.

Tire-repair device. 1,174,254. March 7, 1916. 224:82.

Vehicle-tire. 1,197,030. September 5, 1916. 230:105.

Gravity-railway device. 1,216,694. February 20, 1917. 235:867.

Motion-picture machine. 1,225,636. May 8, 1917. 238:577.

Motion-picture apparatus. 1,229,275. June 12, 1917. 239:353.

Film-handling device. 1,234,545. July 24, 1917. 240:1090.

Lens-holder. 1,258,621. March 5, 1918. 248:197.

Motion-picture machine. 1,281,970. October 15, 1918. 255:564.

Repair device for pneumatic tires. 1,290,566. January 7, 1919. 258:133.

Device for accumulating wave-power. 1,294,808. February 18, 1919. 259:494.

Picture-projecting machine. 1,302,800. May 6, 1919. 262:60.

Motion-picture apparatus. 1,302,801. May 6, 1919. 262:60.

Selective suppression of radiant rays. 1,302,802. May 6, 1919. 262:61.

Picture-film reel. 1,302,803. May 6, 1919. 262:61.

Motion-picture machine. 1,305,804. June 3, 1919. 263:108.

Motion-picture shutter. 1,308,494. July 1, 1919. 264:89.

Motion-picture-projecting apparatus. 1,311,073. July 22, 1919. 264:661.

Film-reel. 1,322,114. November 18, 1919. 268:444.

Picture-projecting apparatus. 1,327,280. January 6, 1920. 270:75.

Flexible reinforced transparent sheet. 1,327,281. January 6, 1920. 270:75.

Motion-picture machine. 1,342,681. June 8, 1920. 275:261.

Film-reel. 1,343,628. June 15, 1920. 275:511.

Limiting combustion of picture-films. 1,348,177. August 3, 1920. 277:9.

Fire-extinguisher for motion-picture apparatus. 1,348,565. August 3, 1920. 277:85.

Motion-picture framing. 1,348,566. August 3, 1920. 277:85.

Electric meter. 1,364,377. January 4, 1921. 282:64.

Motion-picture apparatus. 1,378,462. May 17, 1921. 286:506.

Aeroplane. 1,383,465. July 5, 1921. 288:43.

Motion-picture machine. 1,385,325. July 19, 1921. 288:557.

Producing light-beams. 1,390,445. September 13, 1921. 290:269.

Lawn-mower. 1,401,156. December 27, 1921.

Cooling device for motion-picture machines. 1,408,203. February 28, 1922.

Motion-picture carrier. 1,409,004. March 7, 1922.

Motion-picture device. 1,411,359. April 4, 1922.

Motion-picture apparatus. 1,411,668. April 4, 1922. [With J. N. Ogle.]

Motion-picture mirror of cylindrical type. 1,413,333. April 18, 1922.

Sleevelike refracting prism. 1,440,466. January 2, 1923.

High-speed camera. 1,481,288. January 22, 1924.

Mounting for picture-projecting lights. 1,484,648. February 26, 1924.

Photographing oscillating sparks. 1,521,188. December 30, 1924.

Film reception of broadcasted pictures. 1,521,189. December 30, 1924.

Drum lens carrier. 1,521,190. December 30, 1924.

Prism-lens disk. 1,521,191. December 30, 1924.

Electroscope picture reception. 1,521,192. December 30, 1924.

Pneumatically-controlled light valve. 1,525,548. February 10, 1925.

Radio-picture-frequency chopper. 1,525,549. February 10, 1925.

Flexing mirror. 1,525,550. February 10, 1925.

Magnetically-suspended armature. 1,525,551. February 10, 1925.

Square spotlight source. 1,525,552. February 10, 1925.

Distant motor control. 1,525,553. February 10, 1925.

Radio vision mechanism. 1,530,463. March 17, 1925.

Web-picture-message transmission. 1,533,422. April 14, 1925.

Two-way oscillating mirror. 1,537,087. May 12, 1925.

Device for detecting synchronism. 1,537,088. May 12, 1925.

Objective lens. 1,544,155. June 30, 1925.

Transmitting pictures by wireless. 1,544,156. June 30, 1925.

Radio receiving device. 1,544,157. June 30, 1925.

Wireless broadcasting of pictures. 1,544,158. June 30, 1925.

Double-image radio picture. 1,559,437. October 27, 1925.

Offset filament lamp. 1,572,607. February 9, 1926.

Machine for making optical prisms. 1,573,609. February 16, 1926.

High-speed motion-picture machine. 1,618,090. February 15, 1927.

Airplane stop. 1,634,904. July 5, 1927.

Web message radio. 1,635,324. July 12, 1927.

Film-piercing spark unit. 1,639,775. August 23, 1927.

Multiple light-cell transmitter. 1,641,633. September 6, 1927.

Radio tablet method. 1,642,110. September 13, 1927.

Twin-light-cell transmitter. 1,642,733. September 20, 1927.

Billboard radio picture receiver. 1,643,660. September 27, 1927.

Twin-blade transmitter. 1,644,382. October 4, 1927.

Plural lens-disk analyzer. 1,644,383. October 4, 1927.

Flexing mirror. Reissue 16,767. October 11, 1927.

Apparatus for converting electrical impulses into graphic representations. 1,650,361. November 22, 1927.

Prism-lens disk. Reissue 16,789. November 22, 1927.

Two-way oscillating mirror. Reissue 16,790. November 22, 1927.

Pneumatically-controlled light valve. Reissue 16,818. December 13, 1927.

Radio vision mechanism. Reissue 16,882. February 14, 1928.

Electric transmission of graphic representation. 1,659,200. February 14, 1928.

Radio vision illumination. 1,659,736. February 21, 1928.

Electroscope picture reception. Reissue 16,888. February 21, 1928.

Synchronism in radio movies. 1,660,711. February 28, 1928.

Rotary relay. 1,662,677. March 13, 1928.

Light-concentrating device. 1,663,308. March 20, 1928.

Grid-coupled cell circuit. 1,667,383. April 24, 1928.

Grid-leak cell circuit. 1,667,384. April 24, 1928.

Prism-lens unit. 1,677,590. July 17, 1928.

Spiral-mounted lens disk. 1,679,086. July 31, 1928.

Method of and apparatus for converting light impulses into graphic representations. 1,683,136. September 4, 1928.

Method of and apparatus for converting light impulses into enlarged graphic representations. 1,683,137. September 4, 1928.

Radio vision studio equipment. 1,684,736. September 18, 1928.

High-speed camera. Reissue 17,119. October 30, 1928.

Depth meter. 1,691,719. November 13, 1928.

Picture transmission. 1,693,508. November 27, 1928.

Resistor cell circuit. 1,693,509. November 27, 1928.

Duplex radio-machine. 1,694,065. December 4, 1928.

Reversing-propeller throttle control. 1,694,220. December 4, 1928.

Light-converging-lens system. 1,695,980. December 18, 1928.

Radio movie receiver. 1,697,527. January 1, 1929.

Synchronism in radio movies. Reissue 17, 221. February 19, 1929.

Oscillator cell circuit. 1,704,360. March 5, 1929.

Airplane-launching gear. 1,706,065. March 19, 1929.

Ground-speed meter. 1,711,318. April 30, 1929.

Helical drum scanner. 1,730,976. October 8, 1929.

Spot illumination of lens cells. 1,739, 312. December 10, 1929.

Light-valve transmitter. 1,740,352. December 17, 1929.

Weather-map pen box. 1,740,353. December 17, 1929.

Split switching gear. 1,740,354. December 17, 1929.

Contact scanning disk. 1,740,654. December 24, 1929.

Radio vision analysis. 1,747,173. February 18, 1930.

Controlled-aperture scanning disk. 1,748,383. February 25, 1930.

Cell persistence transmitter. 1,756,291. April 29, 1930.

Altimeter. 1,756,462. April 29, 1930.

Synchronous motor coupling. 1,756,689. April 29, 1930.

Arc-lamp lens-disk transmitter. 1,763,357. June 10, 1930.

Code transmitter receiver. 1,763,358. June 10, 1930.

Synchronizing system. 1,766,644. June 24, 1930.

Loading airplanes. 1,770,700. July 15, 1930.

Grid-leak cell circuit. Reissue 17,766. August 12, 1930.

Method of and apparatus for converting light impulses into enlarged graphic representations. Reissue 17,784. August 26, 1930.

Method of and apparatus for transmitting motion pictures. 1,777,409. October 7, 1930.

Duplex scanning disk. 1,785,262. December 16, 1930.

Airplane-propeller gear. 1,798,740. March 31, 1931.

Scanning device. 1,828,867. October 27, 1931.

Pen-box ink-feed. 1,835,054. December 8, 1931.

Collapsible shutter for projectors. 1,837,776. December 22, 1931.

Cabin airplane ventilation. 1,840,393. January 12, 1932.

Scanning apparatus and method. 1,844,508. February 9, 1932.

Chronoteine or high speed camera. 1,854,742. April 19, 1932.

Spiral mounted lens disk. Reissue 18,425. May 3, 1932.

Aeroplane engine exhaust. 1,858,048. May 10, 1932.

Electrooptical system and method of scanning. 1,859,828. May 24, 1932.

Resistance cell-circuit. 1,879,687. September 27, 1932.

Multiple spot lamp. 1,879,688. September 27, 1932.

Airplane radio equipment. 1,893,287. January 3, 1933.

Gaseous light-valve. 1,894,042. January 10, 1933.

Electric transmission of visual representation. 1,897,481.
February 14, 1933.

Radiomovie lantern slide. 1,899,334. February 28, 1933.

Resistor cell circuit. Reissue 18,756. March 7, 1933.

Synchronizing system. Reissue 18,783. March 28, 1933.

Friction drive. 1,907,116. May 2, 1933.

Multiplex radio communication. 1,914,570. June 20, 1933.

Armature winding. 1,916,374. July 4, 1933.

Incandescent anode lamp. 1,931,658. October 24, 1933.

Mapping camera. 1,939,172. December 12, 1933.

Diathermy contact pad. 1,948,716. February 27, 1934.

Multiplex radiocommunication. 1,957,537. May 8, 1934.

Synchronizing system. Reissue 19,171. May 15, 1934.

Electrooptical device. 1,964,062. June 26, 1934.

Synchronizing system. 1,976,784. October 16, 1934.

Two signal broadcast. 1,976,785. October 16, 1934.

Television scanning device. 1,984,682. December 18, 1934.

Electrooptical system and control. 1,984,683. December 18, 1934.

Two-signal receiving device. 2,017,902. October 22, 1935.

Persisting luminescent screen. 2,021,010. November 12, 1935.

Cell persistence transmitter. Reissue 21, 417. April 2, 1940.

Dynamoelectric machine with distorted field flux. 2,240,652. May 6, 1942.

Fan. 2,240,653. May 6, 1942.

Title Index

Apparatus for making paper bottles. 960,226.
Apparatus for making paper tubes. 1,047,946.
Apparatus for making spirally-wound tubes. 921,842;
    941,255.
Apparatus for providing boxes with closures. 1,047,530.
Apparatus for securing closures in paper tubes. 954,108.
Arc-lamp lens-disk transmitter. 1,763,357.
Armature winding. 1,916,374.
Automatic sign-changing letter. 808,884.
Automobile steering device. 818,967.
Bag-closure. 805,205.
Ball-bearing. 937,811.
Billboard radio picture receiver. 1,643,660.
Blast-furnace. 1,010,265.
Bottle-capping machine. 979,766.
Bottle-closing device. 954,109.
Bottle-filling machine. 828,117.
Box-capping machine. 1,067,431.
Cabin airplane ventilation. 1,840,393.
Cap for bottles. 919,872.
Cell persistence transmitter. 1,756,291.
Cell persistence transmitter. Reissue 21, 417. April 2, 1940.
Chronoteine or high speed camera. 1,854,742.
Closure for paper packages. 943,307.
Closure for paper vessels. 944,615; 993,170.
Closure for receptacles. 970,926.
Closure-making machine. 1,017,549.
Coating paper receptacles. 985,901.
Coating with fusible material. 1,139,291.
Code transmitter receiver. 1,763,358.
Collapsible knockdown box. 947,179.
Collapsible shutter for projectors. 1,837,776.
Contact scanning disk. 1,740,654.
Controlled-aperture scanning disk. 1,748,383.
Cooling device for motion-picture machines. 1,408,203.
Depth meter. 1,691,719.

Device for accumulating wave-power. 1,294,808.
Device for aerial warfare. 1,173,522.
Device for detecting synchronism. 1,537,088.
Device for holding bottle-bodies for the insertion of closures. 958,252.
Device for obtaining stereoscopic effects in exhibiting pictures. 606,993.
Device for underwater exploration. 1,156,782.
Diathermy contact pad. 1,948,716.
Die for making closures for paper bottles. 935,791.
Distant motor control. 1,525,553.
Double-image radio picture. 1,559,437.
Drum lens carrier. 1,521,190.
Duplex radio-machine. 1,694,065.
Duplex scanning disk. 1,785,262.
Dynamoelectric machine with distorted field flux. 2,240,652.
Electric meter. 1,364,377.
Electric transmission of graphic representation. 1,659,200.
Electric transmission of visual representation. 1,897,481.
Electrical contact device. 942,647.
Electrooptical device. 1,964,062.
Electrooptical system and control. 1,984,683.
Electrooptical system and method of scanning. 1,859,828.
Electroscope picture reception. 1,521,192.
Electroscope picture reception. Reissue 16,888. February 21, 1928.
Explosion-engine. 972,380.
Explosion-motor. 972,379.
Fan. 2,240,653.
Film-handling device. 1,234,545.
Film-piercing spark unit. 1,639,775.
Film reception of broadcasted pictures. 1,521,189.
Film-reel. 1,322,114; 1,343,628.
Film-winding device. 1,093,933.
Fire-extinguisher for motion-picture apparatus. 1,348,565.
Flexible reinforced transparent sheet. 1,327,281.

Flexing mirror. 1,525,550.

Flexing mirror. Reissue 16,767. October 11, 1927.

Flying-machine. 1,067,432; 1,081,504; 1,085,263.

Folding box. 941,256; 941,257.

Friction drive. 1,907,116.

Gas-engine starter. 1,047,527.

Gas-motor starter. 1,003,752.

Gaseous light-valve. 1,894,042.

Glue-applying apparatus for box-machines. 985,902.

Gravity-railway device. 1,216,694.

Grid-coupled cell circuit. 1,667,383.

Grid-leak cell circuit. 1,667,384.

Grid-leak cell circuit. Reissue 17,766. August 12, 1930.

Ground-speed meter. 1,711,318.

Heating apparatus. 817,173.

Helical drum scanner. 1,730,976.

High-speed camera. 1,481,288.

High-speed camera. Reissue 17,119. October 30, 1928.

High-speed motion-picture machine. 1,618,090.

Hydrocarbon-burner. 711,925.

Incandescent anode lamp. 1,931,658.

Internal-combustion engine. 1,098,805.

Key and lock. 947,913.

Kinetographic camera. 560,800.

Knockdown box. 944,614; 981,277.

Lawn-mower. 1,401,156.

Lens-holder. 1,258,621.

Light-concentrating device. 1,663,308.

Light-converging-lens system. 1,695,980.

Light-valve transmitter. 1,740,352.

Limiting combustion of picture-films. 1,348,177.

Liquid-holding paper vessel. 920,150.

Loading airplanes. 1,770,700.

Machine for forming and cutting off tubes. 957,966.

Machine for inserting closures in receptacles. 954,106;
    985,900.

Machine for making optical prisms. 1,573,609.
Machine for making paper bottles. 933,460.
Machine for making tubes. 964,162.
Magnetically-suspended armature. 1,525,551.
Mailing-folder. 974,276.
Making boxes or bottles. 991,509.
Making paper bottle-closures. 924,555.
Making paper-tube caps. 860,385.
Making receptacle-closures. 988,716.
Making spirally-wound tubes. 916,162.
Mapping camera. 1,939,172.
Method of and apparatus for converting light impulses into enlarged graphic representations. 1,683,137.
Method of and apparatus for converting light impulses into enlarged graphic representations. Reissue 17,784. August 26, 1930.
Method of and apparatus for converting light impulses into graphic representations. 1,683,136.
Method of and apparatus for transmitting motion pictures. 1,777,409.
Motion-picture apparatus. 865,593; 1,010,370; 1,017,672; 1,047,528; 1,091,343; 1,152,515; 1,153,164; 1,163,757; 1,229,275; 1,302,801; 1,378,462; 1,411,668.
Motion-picture camera. 934,894; 1,089,646.
Motion-picture carrier. 1,409,004.
Motion-picture device. 1,411,359.
Motion-picture framing. 1,348,566.
Motion-picture machine. 819,514; 1,225,636; 1,281,970; 1,305,804; 1,342,681; 1,385,325.
Motion-picture mirror of cylindrical type. 1,413,333.
Motion-picture-projecting apparatus. 1,311,073.
Motion-picture shutter. 1,308,494.
Mounting for picture-projecting lights. 1,484,648.
Moving-picture apparatus. 779,364; 1,083,016.
Multiple light-cell transmitter. 1,641,633.
Multiple spot lamp. 1,879,688.

Multiplex radio communication. 1,914,570.
Multiplex radiocommunication. 1,957,537.
Objective lens. 1,544,155.
Offset filament lamp. 1,572,607.
Oscillator cell circuit. 1,704,360.
Package for chemicals. 949,708.
Package for frangible articles. 944,616.
Paper bottle. 949,036.
Paper-box machinery. 972,767.
Paper package. 925,913.
Paper receptacle. 838,416; 941,992; 944,613; 954,104;
    954,105.
Paper-tube machinery. 984,002.
Paper vessel. 935,029.
Pen-box ink-feed. 1,835,054.
Persisting luminescent screen. 2,021,010.
Phantoscope. 536,569; 586,953.
Photographic-printing apparatus. 649,730.
Photographing oscillating sparks. 1,521,188.
Picture-film rack. 1,045,410.
Picture-film reel. 1,302,803.
Picture-projecting apparatus. 1,153,163; 1,327,280.
Picture-projecting device. 1,090,622.
Picture-projecting machine. 1,302,800.
Picture transmission. 1,693,508.
Plural lens-disk analyzer. 1,644,383.
Pneumatically-controlled light valve. 1,525,548.
Pneumatically-controlled light valve. Reissue 16,818.
    December 13, 1927.
Prism-lens disk. 1,521,191.
Prism-lens disk. Reissue 16,789. November 22, 1927.
Prism-lens unit. 1,677,590.
Producing light-beams. 1,390,445.
Radio movie receiver. 1,697,527.
Radio-picture-frequency chopper. 1,525,549.
Radio receiving device. 1,544,157.

Radio tablet method. 1,642,110.
Radio vision analysis. 1,747,173.
Radio vision illumination. 1,659,736.
Radio vision mechanism. 1,530,463.
Radio vision mechanism. Reissue 16,882. February 14, 1928.
Radio vision studio equipment. 1,684,736.
Radiomovie lantern slide. 1,899,334.
Railway-tie. 1,003,751.
Receptacle for materials to be applied with a brush. 891,262.
Receptacle-labeling apparatus 983,060.
Repair device for pneumatic tires. 1,290,566.
Resistance cell-circuit. 1,879,687.
Resistor cell circuit. 1,693,509.
Resistor cell circuit. Reissue 18,756. March 7, 1933.
Reversing-propeller throttle control. 1,694,220.
Rotary relay. 1,662,677.
Scanning apparatus and method. 1,844,508.
Scanning device. 1,828,867.
Selective suppression of radiant rays. 1,302,802.
Sleevelike refracting prism. 1,440,466.
Spiral-mounted lens disk. 1,679,086.
Spiral mounted lens disk. Reissue 18,425. May 3, 1932.
Spirally-wound collapsible receptacle. 952,258.
Split switching gear. 1,740,354.
Spot illumination of lens cells. 1,739,312.
Square spotlight source. 1,525,552.
Starting device for gas-engines. 1,003,750.
Starting device for internal-combustion engines. 1,024,077.
Steam-generator flue. 926,700; 926,701.
Stereoscopic mutoscope. 671,111.
Synchronism in radio movies. 1,660,711.
Synchronism in radio movies. Reissue 17, 221. February 19, 1929.
Synchronizing system. 1,766,644; 1,976,784.
Synchronizing system. Reissue 18,783. March 28, 1933.
Synchronizing system. Reissue 19,171. May 15, 1934.

Synchronous motor coupling. 1,756,689.
Tapering metal bodies. 1,017,671.
Telautograph. 909,421.
Television scanning device. 1,984,682.
Tire-repair device. 1,024,078; 1,174,254.
Transmitting pictures by wireless. 1,544,156.
Treating paper bottles. 935,848.
Tube-winding device. 982,430.
Twin-blade transmitter. 1,644,382.
Twin-light-cell transmitter. 1,642,733.
Two-cycle gas-engine. 997,195.
Two signal broadcast. 1,976,785.
Two-signal receiving device. 2,017,902.
Two-way oscillating mirror. 1,537,087.
Two-way oscillating mirror. Reissue 16,790. November 22, 1927.
Valve. 1,047,529; 1,047,531.
Vapor-burner. 731,370.
Vehicle-tire. 1,062,011; 1,197,030.
View-changing device. 1,153,110.
Warning-signal. 983,236.
Weather-map pen box. 1,740,353.
Web message radio. 1,635,324.
Web-picture-message transmission. 1,533,422.
Wheel-rim. 1,032,286.
Wireless broadcasting of pictures. 1,544,158.

A. ATWATER KENT (1873-1949)

Electric toy. 671,891. April 9, 1901. 95:404. [With Kendrick and Davis.]

Electric measuring instrument. 764,814. July 12, 1904. 111:428.

Vibrator for induction or spark coils. 783,207. February 21, 1905. 114:2010.

Means for preventing strains and vibrations in power-transmission devices. 798,682. September 5, 1905. 118:59.

Governor. 838,256. December 11, 1906. 125:1892.

Measuring-gage. 922,152. May 18, 1909. 142:738.

Sparking device. 950,339. February 22, 1910. 151:951. [With Thomas H. McQuown.]

Electric contact device. 978,030. December 6, 1910. 161:209.

Massage-machine. 978,031. December 6, 1910. 161:210.

Signaling-horn. 1,001,046. August 22, 1911. 169:735.

Electric-circuit closer and breaker. 1,011,070. December 5, 1911. 173:232. [With Thomas H. McQuown.]

Electric meter. 1,019,163. March 5, 1912. 176:55.

Combined switch and starting device. 1,043,110. November 5, 1912. 184:21.

Electric device. 1,082,810. December 30, 1913. 197:1119.

Device for uniting insulated conductors of electricity. 1,082,811. December 30, 1913. 197:1120.

Circuit-controller. 1,096,109. May 12, 1914. 202:354.

Electric contact device. 1,099,093. June 2, 1914. 203:246.

Electric-circuit closer and breaker. 1,109,689. September 8, 1914. 206:335.

Electric contact device. 1,152,642. September 7, 1915. 218:97.

Signaling-horn. 1,152,643. September 7, 1915. 218:97.

Switch. 1,184,183. May 23, 1916. 226:1212.

Electric contact device. 1,192,786. July 25, 1916. 228:1397.

Automatic spark-advancing mechanism. 1,192,787. July 25, 1916. 228:1397.

Electric igniting mechanism for internal-combustion engines. 1,192,788. July 25, 1916. 228:1398.

Horn. 1,222,107. April 10, 1917. 237:417.

Electric contact device. 1,246,818. November 13, 1917. 244:530.

Circuit make-and-break device. 1,255,846. February 12, 1918. 247:259. [With Walter D. Appel.]

Vehicle-spring. 1,288,915. December 24, 1918. 257:764.

Contact device. 1,289,036. December 24, 1918. 257:792.

Electric igniting mechanism for internal-combustion engines. 1,341,136. May 25, 1920. 274:672.

Condenser unit and making same. 1,351,787. September 7, 1920. 278:14. [With William H. Richter.]

Prismatic telescope. 1,364,381. January 4, 1921. 282:64.

Contact device. Reissue 15,128. June 21, 1921. 287:545.

Induction-coil-heat-dissipating structure. 1,385,624. July 26, 1921. 288:695.

Distributer structure. 1,385,625. July 26, 1921. 288:695.

Ignition timer structure. 1,385,626. July 26, 1921. 288:696.

Induction-coil structure. 1,391,256. September 20, 1921. 290:496.

Electric contact device. 1,395,427. November 1, 1921.

Ignition-control apparatus. 1,407,284. February 21, 1922.

Ignition-control apparatus. 1,407,466. February 21, 1922.

Vehicle seat. 1,417,744. May 30, 1922.

Rheostat. 1,445,324. February 13, 1923.

Engine-starting apparatus. 1,464,714. August 14, 1923.

Induction-coil. 1,474,152. November 13, 1923.

Induction coil. 1,474,597. November 20, 1923.

Ignition apparatus. 1,474,970. November 20, 1923.

Ignition apparatus. 1,476,522. December 4, 1923.

Ignition system for internal-combustion engines. 1,479,388. January 1, 1924. [With W. A. Evans.]

Coupling and tuning apparatus. 1,485,931. March 4, 1924.

Variable-coil structure. 1,514,322. November 4, 1924.

Rheostat. 1,519,621. December 16, 1924.

Condenser and holder therefor. 1,520,027. December 23, 1924.

Variometer. 1,523,832. January 20, 1925.

Rheostat. 1,524,258. January 27, 1925.

Loud speaker. 1,534,267. April 21, 1925.

Ignition apparatus. 1,560,246. November 3, 1925.

Ignition apparatus. 1,560,247. November 3, 1925.

Ignition coil. 1,569,756. January 12, 1926.

Ignition apparatus. 1,570,680. January 26, 1926.

Electric igniting mechanism for internal-combustion engines.
Reissue 16,313. April 6, 1926.

Panel condenser. 1,582,826. April 27, 1926.

Panel condenser. 1,583,071. May 4, 1926.

Panel condenser. 1,583,471. May 4, 1926.

Condenser. 1,588,474. June 15, 1926.

Electromagnetic switch. 1,591,133. July 6, 1926.

Ignition apparatus. 1,591,424. July 6, 1926.

Radio apparatus. 1,597,901. August 31, 1926.

Vacuum-tube unit. 1,650,754. November 29, 1927.

Method and apparatus for producing oscillations. 1,651,012.
November 29, 1927. [With Thomas Appleby.]

Radiocabinet. Design 74,149. December 27, 1927.

Radio apparatus. 1,655,372. January 3, 1928.

Radio receiving apparatus. 1,658,562. February 7, 1928.

Adjustable resistance. 1,668,117. May 1, 1928.

Radio receiving apparatus. 1,668,155. May 1, 1928.

Condenser. 1,668,320. May 1, 1928.

Loud speaker. 1,673,461. June 12, 1928.

Detector apparatus. 1,679,310. July 31, 1928.

Control method and apparatus. 1,683,012. September 4, 1928. [With Thomas Appleby.]

Cabinet for radio receiving apparatus. Design 76,812. November 6, 1928.

Cabinet for radio receiving apparatus. Design 78,030. March 19, 1929.

Radio speaker. 1,705,925. March 19, 1929.

Cabinet. 1,710,482. April 23, 1929.

Condenser. 1,713,134. May 14, 1929.

Radio apparatus. 1,719,014. July 2, 1929.

Transformer. 1,719,057. July 2, 1929.

Method of and apparatus for producing oscillations. 1,719,956. July 9, 1929. [With Thomas Appleby.]

Ignition-governing apparatus. 1,725,522. August 20, 1929.

Loudspeaker. 1,727,604. September 10, 1929.

Vacuum-tube holder. 1,730,010. October 1, 1929.

Radio loud-speaking apparatus. 1,743,145. January 14, 1930.

Loud-speaker mounting. 1,757,719. May 6, 1930.

Ignition-timing apparatus. 1,760,145. May 27, 1930.

Receiving system. 1,775,399. September 9, 1930.

Cabinet for radio receiving apparatus. Design 82,206. September 30, 1930.

Cabinet for radio receiving apparatus. Design 82,207. September 30, 1930.

Radio receiving apparatus. 1,783,292. December 2, 1930.

Radio dial escutcheon plate. Design 83,046. January 13, 1931.

Radiospeaker. 1,794,855. March 3, 1931.

Volume control. 1,796,375. March 17, 1931.

Cabinet for radio receiving apparatus. Design 83,682. March 17, 1931.

Cabinet for radio receiving apparatus. Design 85,244. September 29, 1931.

Radio speaker. 1,829,007. October 27, 1931. [With R. T. Kingsford.]

Anode supply system. 1,972,279. September 4, 1934. [With Sarkes Tarzian.]

Reading apparatus. 2,325,324. July 27, 1943.

Title Index

Adjustable resistance. 1,668,117.
Anode supply system. 1,972,279.
Automatic spark-advancing mechanism. 1,192,787.

Cabinet. 1,710,482.
Cabinet for radio receiving apparatus. Design 76,812.
    November 6, 1928.
Cabinet for radio receiving apparatus. Design 78,030. March
    19, 1929.
Cabinet for radio receiving apparatus. Design 82,206.
    September 30, 1930.
Cabinet for radio receiving apparatus. Design 82,207.
    September 30, 1930.
Cabinet for radio receiving apparatus. Design 83,682. March
    17, 1931.
Cabinet for radio receiving apparatus. Design 85,244.
    September 29, 1931.
Circuit-controller. 1,096,109.
Circuit make-and-break device. 1,255,846.
Combined switch and starting device. 1,043,110.
Condenser. 1,588,474; 1,668,320; 1,713,134.
Condenser and holder therefor. 1,520,027.
Condenser unit and making same. 1,351,787.
Contact device. 1,289,036.
Contact device. Reissue 15,128. June 21, 1921.
Control method and apparatus. 1,683,012.
Coupling and tuning apparatus. 1,485,931.
Detector apparatus. 1,679,310.
Device for uniting insulated conductors of electricity.
    1,082,811.
Distributer structure. 1,385,625.
Electric-circuit closer and breaker. 1,011,070; 1,109,689.
Electric contact device. 978,030; 1,099,093; 1,152,642;
    1,192,786; 1,246,818; 1,395,427.
Electric device. 1,082,810.
Electric igniting mechanism for internal-combustion engines.
    1,192,788; 1,341,136.
Electric igniting mechanism for internal-combustion engines.
    Reissue 16,313. April 6, 1926.
Electric measuring instrument. 764,814.

Electric meter. 1,019,163.
Electric toy. 671,891.
Electromagnetic switch. 1,591,133.
Engine-starting apparatus. 1,464,714.
Governor. 838,256.
Horn. 1,222,107.
Ignition apparatus. 1,474,970; 1,476,522; 1,560,246;
    1,560,247; 1,570,680.
Ignition apparatus. 1,591,424.
Ignition coil. 1,569,756.
Ignition-control apparatus. 1,407,284; 1,407,466.
Ignition-governing apparatus. 1,725,522.
Ignition system for internal-combustion engines. 1,479,388.
Ignition timer structure. 1,385,626.
Ignition-timing apparatus. 1,760,145.
Induction-coil. 1,474,152; 1,474,597.
Induction-coil-heat-dissipating structure. 1,385,624.
Induction-coil structure. 1,391,256.
Loud speaker. 1,534,267; 1,673,461; 1,727,604.
Loud-speaker mounting. 1,757,719.
Massage-machine. 978,031.
Means for preventing strains and vibrations in power-
    transmission devices. 798,682.
Measuring-gage. 922,152.
Method and apparatus for producing oscillations. 1,651,012.
Method of and apparatus for producing oscillations.
    1,719,956.
Panel condenser. 1,582,826; 1,583,071; 1,583,471.
Prismatic telescope. 1,364,381.
Radio apparatus. 1,597,901; 1,655,372; 1,719,014.
Radio dial escutcheon plate. Design 83,046. January 13, 1931.
Radio loud-speaking apparatus. 1,743,145.
Radio receiving apparatus. 1,658,562; 1,668,155; 1,783,292.
Radio speaker. 1,705,925; 1,829,007.
Radiocabinet. Design 74,149. December 27, 1927.
Radiospeaker. 1,794,855.

Reading apparatus. 2,325,324.
Receiving system. 1,775,399.
Rheostat. 1,445,324; 1,519,621; 1,524,258.
Signaling-horn. 1,001,046; 1,152,643.
Sparking device. 950,339.
Switch. 1,184,183.
Transformer. 1,719,057.
Vacuum-tube holder. 1,730,010.
Vacuum-tube unit. 1,650,754.
Variable-coil structure. 1,514,322.
Variometer. 1,523,832.
Vehicle seat. 1,417,744.
Vehicle-spring. 1,288,915.
Vibrator for induction or spark coils. 783,207.
Volume control. 1,796,375.

SAMUEL KINTNER (1871-1936)

Separating liquids. 854,295. May 21, 1907. 128:1070. [With W. W. Hanks.]

Means for cooling transformers. 854,312. May 21, 1907. 128:1078. [With C. E. Skinner.]

Ozone-producer. 920,965. May 11, 1909. 142:316.

Fuse-receptacle. 933,787. September 14, 1909. 146:278. [With B. P. Rowe.]

Railway-motor. 947,338. January 25, 1910. 150:875.

Insulating-bushing. 952,448. March 22, 1910. 152:742.

Electrical measuring instrument. 959,551. May 31, 1910. 154:1152.

Fuse for electrical circuits. 959,552. May 31, 1910. 154:1153.

Electrical measuring instrument. 999,800. August 8, 1911. 169:236.

Contact for electromagnetic mechanism. 1,048,670. December 31, 1912. 185:1131. [With R. A. Fessenden and H. M. Barrett.]

Electric signaling apparatus. 1,050,441. January 14, 1913. 186:417. [With R. A. Fessenden and H. M. Barrett.]

Signaling. 1,050,728. January 14, 1913. 186:512. [With R. A. Fessenden and H. M. Barrett.]

Wireless telegraphy. 1,059,665. April 22, 1913. 189:898. [With R. A. Fessenden and H. M. Barrett.]

Apparatus for wireless signaling. 1,059,666. April 22, 1913. 189:898. [With R. A. Fessenden and H. M. Barrett.]

Resister [sic]. 1,068,907. July 29, 1913. 192:1173. [With Paul Kraeuter.]

Wireless signaling. 1,074,423. September 30, 1913. 194:1064. [With R. A. Fessenden and H. M. Barrett.]

Magnetic material. 1,074,424. September 30, 1913. 194:1064. [With R. A. Fessenden and H. M. Barrett.]

Signaling by electromagnetic waves. 1,080,271. December 2, 1913. 197:124. [With R. A. Fessenden and H. M. Barrett.]

Apparatus for electric signaling. 1,101,914. June 30, 1914. 203:1404. [With R. A. Fessenden and H. M. Barrett.]

Wireless signaling. 1,101,915. June 30, 1914. 203:1405. [With R. A. Fessenden and H. M. Barrett.]

Sending mechanism for electromagnetic waves. 1,126,966. February 2, 1915. 211:105. [With R. A. Fessenden and H. M. Barrett.]

Electric signaling. 1,132,568. March 23, 1915. 212:1077. [With R. A. Fessenden and H. M. Barrett.]

Wireless telegraphy. 1,132,569. March 23, 1915. 212:1077. [With R. A. Fessenden and H. M. Barrett.]

Wireless-telegraph receiving apparatus. 1,132,588. March 23, 1915. 212:1085. [With J. W. Lee and H. M. Barrett.]

Spark-gap. 1,132,589. March 23, 1915. 212:1085. [With F. H. Kroger and H. M. Barrett.]

Bearing-housing. 1,138,666. May 11, 1915. 214:368.

Transmitting and receiving electrical energy. 1,141,386. June 1, 1915. 215:108. [With R. A. Fessenden and H. M. Barrett.]

Apparatus for the transmission and receipt of electrical energy. 1,141,453. June 1, 1915. 215:131. [With R. A. Fessenden and H. M. Barrett.]

Transmitting intelligence by radiant energy. 1,141,717. June 1, 1915. 215:223. [With J. W. Lee, J. L. Hogan, and H. M. Barrett.]

Wireless telegraphy. 1,147,010. July 20, 1915. 216:753. [With R. A. Fessenden and H. M. Barrett.]

Oscillating-current meter. 1,152,632. September 7, 1915. 218:93. [With John L. Hogan, Jr., and H. M. Barrett.]

Apparatus for transmission of energy by electric oscillations. 1,156,677. October 12, 1915. 219:497. [With R. A. Fessenden and H. M. Barrett.]

Transmitting and receiving signals. 1,157,094. October 19, 1915. 219:673. [With R. A. Fessenden and H. M. Barrett.]

Detector for oscillating currents. 1,158,112. October 26, 1915. 219:1093. [With W. E. Beakes and H. M. Barrett.]

Apparatus for generating and receiving electromagnetic waves. 1,158,123. October 26, 1915. 219:1097. [With R. A. Fessenden and H. M. Barrett.]

Signaling apparatus for aerial navigation. 1,158,124. October 26, 1915. 219:1097. [With R. A. Fessenden and H. M. Barrett.]

Frequency-meter for measuring electrical current. 1,165,850. December 28, 1915. 221:1212. [With L. Cohen and H. M. Barrett.]

Apparatus for wireless signaling. 1,165,862. December 28, 1915. 221:1217. [With R. A. Fessenden and H. M. Barrett.]

Apparatus for producing high-frequency oscillations. 1,166,892. January 4, 1916. 222:167. [With R. A. Fessenden and H. M. Barrett.]

Means of transmitting intelligence. 1,170,969. February 8, 1916. 223:458. [With R. A. Fessenden and H. M. Barrett.]

Transmitting energy by electromagnetic waves. 1,172,017. February 15, 1916. 223:875. [With R. A. Fessenden and H. M. Barrett.]

Electromagnetic indicator. 1,172,018. February 15, 1916. 223:875. [With R. A. Fessenden and H. M. Barrett.]

Wireless telegraphy. 1,175,418. March 14, 1916. 224:530. [With R. A. Fessenden and H. M. Barrett.]

Wireless signaling. 1,176,282. March 21, 1916. 224:872. [With R. A. Fessenden and H. M. Barrett.]

Wireless signaling. 1,178,507. April 11, 1916. 225:835.
[With R. A. Fessenden and H. M. Barrett.]

Electric signaling. 1,179,906. April 18, 1916. 225:932. [With
R. A. Fessenden and H. M. Barrett.]

Signaling by electromagnetic waves. 1,182,003. May 9, 1916.
226:353. [With R. A. Fessenden and H. M. Barrett.]

Wireless-telegraph detector. 1,182,946. May 16, 1916.
226:727. [With R. J. Vosburgh and H. M. Barrett.]

Spark-gap. 1,192,909. August 1, 1916. 229:27. [With F. H.
Kroger and H. M. Barrett.]

Oscillating-current transformer. 1,192,964. August 1, 1916.
229:46. [With R. A. Weagant and H. M. Barrett.]

Method and apparatus for amplifying electric impulses.
1,196,938. September 5, 1916. 230:72. [With R. A.
Fessenden, L. Cohen, and H. M. Barrett.]

Receiver for wireless telegraphy. 1,363,319. December 28,
1920. 281:600. [With J. L. Hogan and H. M. Barrett.]

Speed governor. 1,409,553. March 14, 1922.

System of control. 1,502,831. July 29, 1924.

Polyphase plate-circuit-excitation system. 1,513,324. October
28, 1924.

Speed-control system for high-frequency generators.
1,669,524. May 15, 1928.

Television apparatus. 1,695,924. December 18, 1928.

Triode tube. 1,700,896. February 5, 1929.

Photo-sensitive apparatus. 1,958,893. May 15, 1934. [With P. Thomas.]

Title Index

Apparatus for electric signaling. 1,101,914.
Apparatus for generating and receiving electromagnetic waves. 1,158,123.
Apparatus for producing high-frequency oscillations. 1,166,892.
Apparatus for the transmission and receipt of electrical energy. 1,141,453.
Apparatus for transmission of energy by electric oscillations. 1,156,677.
Apparatus for wireless signaling. 1,059,666; 1,165,862.
Bearing-housing. 1,138,666.
Contact for electromagnetic mechanism. 1,048,670.
Detector for oscillating currents. 1,158,112.
Electric signaling. 1,132,568; 1,179,906.
Electric signaling apparatus. 1,050,441.
Electrical measuring instrument. 959,551; 999,800.
Electromagnetic indicator. 1,172,018.
Frequency-meter for measuring electrical current. 1,165,850.
Fuse for electrical circuits. 959,552.
Fuse-receptacle. 933,787.
Insulating-bushing. 952,448.
Magnetic material. 1,074,424.
Means for cooling transformers. 854,312.
Means of transmitting intelligence. 1,170,969.
Method and apparatus for amplifying electric impulses. 1,196,938.
Oscillating-current meter. 1,152,632.
Oscillating-current transformer. 1,192,964.

Ozone-producer. 920,965.

Photo-sensitive apparatus. 1,958,893.

Polyphase plate-circuit-excitation system. 1,513,324.

Railway-motor. 947,338.

Receiver for wireless telegraphy. 1,363,319.

Resister [sic]. 1,068,907.

Sending mechanism for electromagnetic waves. 1,126,966.

Separating liquids. 854,295.

Signaling. 1,050,728.

Signaling apparatus for aerial navigation. 1,158,124.

Signaling by electromagnetic waves. 1,080,271; 1,182,003.

Spark-gap. 1,132,589; 1,192,909.

Speed-control system for high-frequency generators.
    1,669,524.

Speed governor. 1,409,553.

System of control. 1,502,831.

Television apparatus. 1,695,924.

Transmitting and receiving electrical energy. 1,141,386.

Transmitting and receiving signals. 1,157,094.

Transmitting energy by electromagnetic waves. 1,172,017.

Transmitting intelligence by radiant energy. 1,141,717.

Triode tube. 1,700,896.

Wireless signaling. 1,074,423; 1,101,915; 1,176,282;
    1,178,507.

Wireless-telegraph detector. 1,182,946.

Wireless-telegraph receiving apparatus. 1,132,588.

Wireless telegraphy. 1,059,665; 1,132,569; 1,147,010;
    1,175,418.

FREDERICK KOLSTER (1883-1950)

[Note: Patents assigned to Kolster Radio, Inc., but not in Kolster's name are not listed.]

Radio method and apparatus. 1,311,654. July 29, 1919. 264:802.

Apparatus for transmitting radiant energy. 1,394,560. October 25, 1921.

Radio method and apparatus. 1,447,165. February 27, 1923.

Radio-receiving method and apparatus. 1,464,322. August 7, 1923.

Radio signaling system. 1,587,657. June 8, 1926.

Radio method and apparatus. 1,597,379. August 24, 1926.

Radio apparatus. 1,609,366. December 7, 1926.

Radio receiving apparatus. 1,636,570. July 19, 1927.

Electromagnetic sound reproducer. 1,637,119. July 26, 1927. [With S. A. Sollie.]

Radiocompass. 1,637,615. August 2, 1927.

Electron-tube apparatus. 1,637,864. August 2, 1927.

Multiple variable condenser. 1,641,593. September 6, 1927.

Loop antenna. 1,673,249. June 12, 1928.

Loud-speaker system. 1,675,031. June 26, 1928.

Radio receiving system. 1,683,080. September 4, 1928.

Variable-coupling transformer. 1,683,081. September 4, 1928.

Variable condenser. 1,683,558. September 4, 1928.

Electromagnetic sound reproducer. Reissue 17,086. September 18, 1928. [With S. A. Sollie.]

Signal-receiving circuits. 1,707,440. April 2, 1929.

Signal-receiving circuits. 1,708,182. April 9, 1929.

Sound-reproducer. 1,712,920. May 14, 1929.

Radio receiving system. 1,716,352. June 4, 1929.

Selector and receiver for radio frequency energy. 1,717,455. June 18, 1929.

Bearing-coil housing. 1,722,051. July 23, 1929.

Radio compass compensator. 1,725,147. August 20, 1929.

Radio apparatus. 1,726,705. September 3, 1929.

Bearing-coil housing. 1,727,608. September 10, 1929.

Radio apparatus. 1,730,577. October 8, 1929.

Signaling system. 1,737,089. November 26, 1929.

Vacuum-tube system. 1,738,495. December 3, 1929.

Selector system. 1,742,602. January 7, 1930.

Electrical tuning system. 1,743,039. January 7, 1930.

Directional radio system. 1,749,348. March 4, 1930.

Radiocompass. 1,759,119. May 20, 1930.

High-frequency coupling unit. 1,766,039. June 24, 1930.

Signal-transmitting system. 1,766,040. June 24, 1930.

Radio apparatus and method. 1,766,041. June 24, 1930.

Sound-reproducing system. 1,766,046. June 24, 1930. [With J. O. Prescott.]

Radio compass indicator. 1,767,140. June 24, 1930.

Radio compass system. 1,767,141. June 24, 1930.

Radio transmitting system. 1,767,245. June 24, 1930.

Signal-receiving system. 1,787,582. January 6, 1931. [With G. G. Kruesi.]

Radio transmission system. 1,792,746. February 17, 1931.

Radiocompass. 1,800,454. April 14, 1931.

Indicator. 1,800,455. April 14, 1931.

Electrical coupling system. 1,801,352. April 21, 1931.

Directional radio system. 1,806,577. May 19, 1931.

Radio compass. 1,807,919. June 2, 1931.

Antenna system and method. 1,821,649. September 1, 1931. [with G. G. Kruesi.]

Radio system. 1,821,650. September 1, 1931.

Radio system. 1,828,705. October 20, 1931.

Oscillation generator and method. 1,828,706. October 20, 1931. [With G. G. Kruesi.]

Radio receiving system. 1,830,948. November 10, 1931.

Radio beacon system. 1,831,011. November 10, 1931.

Relay system and method. 1,834,283. December 1, 1931.

Radio receiving system. 1,843,565. February 2, 1932.

Loud-speaker. 1,864,308. June 21, 1932. [With S. A. Sollie.]

Electromagnetic sound reproducer system. 1,868,607. July 26, 1932.

Navigation system and method. 1,872,975. August 23, 1932.

Refrigerating system. 1,995,124. March 19, 1935.

High frequency apparatus. 2,019,611. November 5, 1935.

High frequency circuit. 2,031,490. February 18, 1936.

High frequency oscillation generator. 2,068,990. January 26, 1937. [With P. F. Byrne.]

High frequency apparatus. 2,068,991. January 26, 1937.

High frequency circuits. 2,085,223. June 29, 1937.

High frequency amplifier system. 2,089,270. August 10, 1937.

Electrical coupling system. 2,089,271. August 10, 1937.

Ultra-high-frequency radio transmitter. 2,145,225. January 24, 1939. [With P. F. Byrne.]

Temperature compensated high-Q lines or circuits. 2,173,908. September 26, 1939.

Ultra short wave course beacon. 2,212,238. August 20, 1940.

Directional radio system. 2,216,708. October 1, 1940.

High frequency wave transmission system. 2,236,102. March 25, 1941.

Radio direction finding system. 2,463,286. March 1, 1949.

Double superheterodyne radio receiver. 2,534,606. December 19, 1950.

Broad-band antenna system. 2,580,798. January 1, 1952.

Multiband antenna system. 2,619,596. November 25, 1952.

Title Index

Antenna system and method. 1,821,649.

Apparatus for transmitting radiant energy. 1,394,560.

Bearing-coil housing. 1,722,051; 1,727,608.

Broad-band antenna system. 2,580,798.

Directional radio system. 1,749,348; 1,806,577; 2,216,708.

Double superheterodyne radio receiver. 2,534,606.

Electrical coupling system. 1,801,352; 2,089,271.

Electrical tuning system. 1,743,039.

Electromagnetic sound reproducer. 1,637,119.

Electromagnetic sound reproducer. Reissue 17,086. September 18, 1928.

Electromagnetic sound reproducer system. 1,868,607.

Electron-tube apparatus. 1,637,864.

High frequency amplifier system. 2,089,270.

High frequency apparatus. 2,019,611; 2,068,991.

High frequency circuit. 2,031,490.

High frequency circuits. 2,085,223.

High-frequency coupling unit. 1,766,039.

High frequency oscillation generator. 2,068,990.

High frequency wave transmission system. 2,236,102.

Indicator. 1,800,455.

Loop antenna. 1,673,249.

Loud-speaker. 1,864,308.

Loud-speaker system. 1,675,031.

Multiband antenna system. 2,619,596.

Multiple variable condenser. 1,641,593.

Navigation system and method. 1,872,975.

Oscillation generator and method. 1,828,706.

Radio apparatus. 1,609,366; 1,726,705; 1,730,577.

Radio apparatus and method. 1,766,041.

Radio beacon system. 1,831,011.

Radio compass. 1,807,919.

Radio compass compensator. 1,725,147.

Radio compass indicator. 1,767,140.

Radio compass system. 1,767,141.
Radio direction finding system. 2,463,286.
Radio method and apparatus. 1,311,654; 1,447,165;
   1,597,379.
Radio receiving apparatus. 1,636,570.
Radio-receiving method and apparatus. 1,464,322.
Radio receiving system. 1,683,080; 1,716,352; 1,830,948;
   1,843,565.
Radio signaling system. 1,587,657.
Radio system. 1,821,650; 1,828,705.
Radio transmission system. 1,792,746.
Radio transmitting system. 1,767,245.
Radiocompass. 1,637,615; 1,759,119; 1,800,454.
Refrigerating system. 1,995,124.
Relay system and method. 1,834,283.
Selector and receiver for radio frequency energy. 1,717,455.
Selector system. 1,742,602.
Signal-receiving circuits. 1,707,440; 1,708,182.
Signal-receiving system. 1,787,582.
Signal-transmitting system. 1,766,040.
Signaling system. 1,737,089.
Sound-reproducer. 1,712,920.
Sound-reproducing system. 1,766,046.
Temperature compensated high-Q lines or circuits. 2,173,908.
Ultra-high-frequency radio transmitter. 2,145,225.
Ultra short wave course beacon. 2,212,238.
Vacuum-tube system. 1,738,495.
Variable condenser. 1,683,558.
Variable-coupling transformer. 1,683,081.

MAHLON LOOMIS (1826-1886)

Plates for artificial teeth. 10,847. May 2, 1854.

Plate for artificial teeth. (Extension) April 8, 1868.

Telegraphing. 129,971. July 30, 1872. 2:183.

Convertible valise. 241,387. May 10, 1881. 19:1197.

Cuff and collar fastening. 250,268. November 29, 1881. 20:1573.

Electrical thermostat. 338,090. March 16, 1886. 34:1232.

GUGLIELMO MARCONI (1874-1937)

Transmitting electrical signals. 586,193. July 13, 1897.
80:222.

Apparatus employed in wireless telegraphy. 624,516. May 9,
1899. 87:926.

Apparatus employed in wireless telegraphy. 627,650. June 27,
1899. 87:2195.

Apparatus employed in wireless telegraphy. 647,007. April
10, 1900. 91:268.

Apparatus employed in wireless telegraphy. 647,008. April
10, 1900. 91:269.

Apparatus employed in wireless telegraphy. 647,009. April
10, 1900. 91:270.

Apparatus employed in wireless telegraphy. 650,109. May 22,
1900. 91:1515.

Apparatus employed in wireless telegraphy. 650,110. May 22,
1900. 91:1516.

Receiver for electrical oscillations. 668,315. February 19,
1901. 94:1454.

Transmitting electrical impulses and signals and apparatus
therefor. Reissue 11,913. June 4, 1901. 95:2047.

Apparatus for wireless telegraphy. 676,332. June 11, 1901. 95:2257.

Wireless-telegraph system. 757,559. April 19, 1904. 109:1950.

Wireless signaling system. 760,463. May 24, 1904. 110:890.

Apparatus for wireless telegraphy. 763,772. June 28, 1904. 110:2423.

Wireless telegraphy. 786,132. March 28, 1905. 115:1006.

Wireless telegraphy. 792,528. June 13, 1905. 116:1954.

Wireless telegraphy. 884,986. April 14, 1908. 133:1647.

Wireless telegraphy. 884,987. April 14, 1908. 133:1647.

Detecting electrical oscillations. 884,988. April 14, 1908. 133:1648.

Wireless telegraphy. 884,989. April 14, 1908. 133:1648.

Receiver for wireless telegraphy. 896,130. August 18, 1908. 135:1383.

Wireless signaling system. 924,168. June 8, 1909. 143:384.

Wireless signaling system. 924,560. June 8, 1909. 143:513.

Transmitting apparatus for wireless telegraphy. 935,381. September 28, 1909. 146:856.

Apparatus for wireless telegraphy. 935,382. September 28, 1909. 146:856.

Apparatus for wireless telegraphy. 935,383. September 28, 1909. 146:856.

Apparatus for wireless telegraphy. 954,640. April 12, 1910. 153:357.

Wireless telegraphy. 954,641. April 12, 1910. 153:357.

Transmitting apparatus for wireless telegraphy. 997,308. July 11, 1911. 168:274.

Means for generating alternating electric currents. 1,102,990. July 7, 1914. 204:265.

Duplex wireless telegraphy. 1,116,309. November 3, 1914. 208:286.

Transmitting apparatus for use in wireless telegraphy and telephony. 1,136,477. April 20, 1915. 213:931.

Transmitter for wireless telegraphy. 1,148,521. August 3, 1915. 217:13.

Transmitting apparatus for use in wireless telegraphy and telephony. 1,226,099. May 15, 1917. 238:777.

Transformer for high-frequency currents. 1,246,973. November 20, 1917. 244:612.

Wireless-telegraph transmitter. 1,271,190. July 2, 1918. 252:124.

Reflector for use in wireless telegraphy and telephony. 1,301,473. April 22, 1919. 261:713. [With C. S. Franklin.]

Electric accumulator. 1,377,722. May 10, 1921. 286:312.

Thermionic valve. 1,981,058. November 20, 1934. [With
C. S. Franklin.]

Title Index

Apparatus for wireless telegraphy. 676,332; 763,772;
935,382; 935,383; 954,640.
Apparatus employed in wireless telegraphy. 624,516; 627,650;
647,007; 647;008; 647,009; 650,109; 650,110.
Detecting electrical oscillations. 884,988.
Duplex wireless telegraphy. 1,116,309.
Electric accumulator. 1,377,722.
Means for generating alternating electric currents. 1,102,990.
Receiver for electrical oscillations. 668,315.
Receiver for wireless telegraphy. 896,130.
Reflector for use in wireless telegraphy and telephony.
    1,301,473.
Thermionic valve. 1,981,058.
Transformer for high-frequency currents. 1,246,973.
Transmitter for wireless telegraphy. 1,148,521.
Transmitting apparatus for use in wireless telegraphy and
    telephony. 1,136,477; 1,226,099.
Transmitting apparatus for wireless telegraphy. 935,381;
    997,308.
Transmitting electrical signals. 586,193.
Transmitting electrical impulses and signals and apparatus
    therefor. Reissue 11,913. June 4, 1901.
Wireless signaling system. 760,463; 924,168; 924,560.
Wireless-telegraph system. 757,559.
Wireless-telegraph transmitter. 1,271,190.
Wireless telegraphy. 786,132; 792,528; 884,986; 884,987;
    884,989; 954,641.

HIRAM P. MAXIM (1869-1936)

[Note: Patents assigned to the Maxim Silencer Company but not in Maxim's name are not listed.]

Motor vehicle. 594,805. November 30, 1897. 81:1594.

Governor for explosive-engines. 606,425. June 28, 1898. 83:1905.

Explosive-engine. 620,602. March 7, 1899. 86:1520.

Driving mechanism for vehicles. 621,532. March 21, 1899. 86:1882. [With H. M. Pope and H. W. Alden.]

Device for indicating condition of storage batteries. 640,787. January 9, 1900. 90:253.

Valve-gear for explosive-motors. 645,177. March 13, 1900. 90:2000. [With M. Pope.]

Vehicle-frame. 647,505. April 17, 1900. 91:486. [With M. Pope.]

Electric cut-out. 653,685. July 17, 1900. 92:398.

Running-frame for vehicles. 657,430. September 4, 1900. 92:1939.

Signal-actuating apparatus. 676,584. June 18, 1901. 95:2366.

Detachable traction-strap. 681,173. August 20, 1901. 96:1631.

Motor-vehicle. 699,543. May 6, 1902. 99:1334.

Motor-vehicle. 702,448. June 17, 1902. 99:2579.

Steering mechanism for vehicles. 702,980. June 24, 1902. 99:2809.

Motor-vehicle. 716,917. December 30, 1902. 101:2853.

Charge-indicator for secondary batteries. 731,484. June 23, 1903. 104:1930.

Charging system for secondary batteries. 742,886. November 3, 1903. 107:26.

Electric motor. 751,191. February 2, 1904. 108:1219.

Electrically-propelled vehicle. 753,284. March 1, 1904. 109:32.

Traction-strap. 753,285. March 1, 1904. 109:33.

Vehicle-brake. 757,940. April 19, 1904. 109:2114.

Motor-vehicle running-gear. 757,941. April 19, 1904. 109:2115.

Motor suspension for vehicles. 760,747. May 24, 1904. 110:1019.

Gearing. 764,896. July 12, 1904. 111:464.

Electric motor-vehicle. 772,571. October 18, 1904. 112:1590.

Tire for vehicles. 798,815. September 5, 1905. 118:116.

Axle-end. 801,804. October 10, 1905. 118:1647. [With H. W. Alden.]

Motor road-vehicle. 845,106. February 26, 1907. 126:3088.

Generation of vapor. 865,725. September 10, 1907. 130:439. [With Harry M. Pope.]

Silent firearm. 880,386. February 25, 1908. 132:1770.

Silent firearm. 916,885. March 30, 1909. 140:1162.

Sand-box for rifle practice. 941,642. November 30, 1909. 148:1187.

Tire-inflater for automobiles. 956,592. May 3, 1910. 154:32.

Silent firearm. 958,934. May 24, 1910. 154:921.

Silent firearm. 958,935. May 24, 1910. 154:922.

Gas engine silencer. 1,015,698. January 23, 1912. 174:981.

Silencing device for firearms. 1,018,720. February 27, 1912. 175:958.

Automobile-starter. 1,020,106. March 12, 1912. 176:401.

Motor-vehicle. 1,021,061. March 26, 1912. 176:810.

Firearm. 1,054,434. February 25, 1913. 187:999.

Control-lever lock for motor-vehicles. 1,057,865. April 1, 1913. 189:161.

Silencer for gas-engines, &c. 1,060,925. May 6, 1913.
190:125.

Axle for motor-vehicles. 1,097,866. May 26, 1914. 202:1049.

Driving-gear for motor-vehicles. 1,103,978. July 21, 1914.
204:698.

Silencer for gas-engines, &c. 1,111,265. September 22, 1914.
206:974.

Silencer for gas-engines, &c. 1,114,701. October 20, 1914.
207:882.

Silencer for gas-engines, &c. 1,114,702. October 20, 1914.
207:883.

Exhaust-silencer for engines. 1,115,853. November 3, 1914.
208:131.

Scabbard. 1,276,554. August 20, 1918. 253:674.

Building-silencer. 1,289,856. December 31, 1918. 257:1020.

Silencer. 1,330,486. February 10, 1920. 271:244.

Silencer for guns. 1,482,805. February 5, 1924.

Muffler. 1,547,601. June 28, 1925.

Silencer. 1,584,315. May 11, 1926.

Silencer. 1,598,578. August 31, 1926.

Silencer. 1,601,136. September 28, 1926.

Silencer. 1,601,137. September 28, 1926.

Silencer. 1,611,475. December 21, 1926.

Silencer. 1,636,238. July 19, 1927.

Silencer. 1,637,385. August 2, 1927.

Silencer. 1,639,047. August 16, 1927.

Silencer. 1,695,435. December 18, 1928.

Silencer. 1,705,528. March 19, 1929.

Silencer. 1,709,992. April 23, 1929.

Silencer. Reissue 17,299. May 21, 1929.

Silencer. 1,732,943. October 22, 1929. [With R. B. Bourne.]

Silencer. 1,736,319. November 19, 1929.

Silencer. 1,756,297. April 29, 1930. [With R. B. Bourne.]

Title Index

Automobile-starter. 1,020,106.
Axle-end. 801,804.
Axle for motor-vehicles. 1,097,866.
Building-silencer. 1,289,856.
Charge-indicator for secondary batteries. 731,484.
Charging system for secondary batteries. 742,886.
Control-lever lock for motor-vehicles. 1,057,865.
Detachable traction-strap. 681,173.
Device for indicating condition of storage batteries. 640,787.

Driving-gear for motor-vehicles. 1,103,978.
Driving mechanism for vehicles. 621,532.
Electric cut-out. 653,685.
Electric motor. 751,191.
Electric motor-vehicle. 772,571.
Electrically-propelled vehicle. 753,284.
Exhaust-silencer for engines. 1,115,853.
Explosive-engine. 620,602.
Firearm. 1,054,434.
Gas engine silencer. 1,015,698.
Gearing. 764,896.
Generation of vapor. 865,725.
Governor for explosive-engines. 606,425.
Motor road-vehicle. 845,106.
Motor suspension for vehicles. 760,747.
Motor vehicle. 594,805; 699,543; 702,448; 716,917;
    1,021,061.
Motor-vehicle running-gear. 757,941.
Muffler. 1,547,601.
Running-frame for vehicles. 657,430.
Sand-box for rifle practice. 941,642.
Scabbard. 1,276,554.
Signal-actuating apparatus. 676,584.
Silencer. 1,330,486; 1,584,315; 1,598,578; 11,601,136;
    1,601,137; 1,611,475; 1,636,238; 1,637,385; 1,639,047;
    1,695,435; 1,705,528; 1,709,992; 1,732,943; 1,736,319;
    1,756,297.
Silencer. Reissue 17,299. May 21, 1929.
Silencer for gas-engines, &c. 1,060,925; 1,111,265;
    1,114,701; 1,114,702.
Silencer for guns. 1,482,805.
Silencing device for firearms. 1,018,720.
Silent firearm. 880,386; 916,885; 958,934; 958,935.
Steering mechanism for vehicles. 702,980.
Tire for vehicles. 798,815.
Tire-inflater for automobiles. 956,592.

Traction-strap. 753,285.
Valve-gear for explosive-motors. 645,177.
Vehicle-brake. 757,940.
Vehicle-frame. 647,505.

BENJAMIN MIESSNER (1890-1976)

Detector for wireless apparatus. 1,104,065. July 21, 1914. 204:728.

Electric music-chart. 1,268,376. June 4, 1918. 251:87. [With W. O. Miessner.]

Speaking-tube apparatus for aircraft. 1,418,388. June 6, 1922.

Sound amplifier. Design 64,507. April 22, 1924.

Sound amplifier. Design 64,508. April 22, 1924.

Telephone transmitter. 1,507,081. September 2, 1924.

Electronic telephone. 1,593,636. July 27, 1926.

Radio communication device. 1,622,389. March 29, 1927.

Sound amplifying device. 1,639,048. August 16, 1927.

Musical instrument. 1,698,958. January 15, 1929.

Electron-discharge device. 1,718,059. June 18, 1929.

Electrical signal amplifying and repeating system. 1,719,189. July 2, 1929.

Electrical signal-amplifying system. 1,720,914. July 16, 1929.

Microphone. 1,722,851. July 30, 1929.

Electromagnetic translating device. 1,728,278. September 17, 1929.

Signal-lamp mounting. 1,729,080. September 24, 1929.

Electrodynamic sound-reproducing system. 1,733,232. October 29, 1929.

Electrical supply and filter system. 1,788,342. January 6, 1931.

Electrical signal amplifying and repeating system. 1,789,950. January 20, 1931.

Electrical amplifier system. 1,790,874. February 3, 1931.

Electron tube energizing method and apparatus. 1,806,813. May 26, 1931.

Method of and apparatus for changing voltage. 1,823,837. September 15, 1931.

Electromagnetic sound reproducer. 1,830,401. November 3, 1931.

Electromagnetic sound reproducer. 1,830,402. November 3, 1931.

Unidirectional current system. 1,832,646. November 17, 1931.

Electron discharge apparatus. 1,834,131. December 1, 1931.

Electrical amplifying system. 1,834,414. December 1, 1931.

Amplifier energizing system. 1,842,558. January 26, 1932.

Radio receiving system. 1,842,977. January 26, 1932.

Electrical filter system. 1,852,125. April 5, 1932.

Electrical filter system. 1,853,217. April 12, 1932.

Amplifier system. 1,854,854. April 19, 1932.

Electron tube. 1,859,454. May 24, 1932.

Electron tube. 1,859,522. May 24, 1932.

Electron tube. 1,890,911. December 13, 1932.

Method and apparatus for the production of music. 1,912,293. May 30, 1933.

Electrical supply system. 1,912,991. June 6, 1933.

Method and apparatus for the production of music. 1,915,858. June 27, 1933.

Method and apparatus for the production of music. 1,915,859. June 27, 1933. [With C. T. Jacobs.]

Method and apparatus for the production of music. 1,915,860. June 27, 1933. [With C. T. Jacobs.]

Discharge tube cathode energizing. 1,917,728. July 11, 1933.

Electrical filter system. 1,927,689. September 19, 1933.

Method and apparatus for the production of music. 1,929,027. October 3, 1933.

Method and apparatus for the production of music. 1,929,028. October 3, 1933.

Apparatus for the production of music. 1,929,029. October 3, 1933.

Apparatus for the production of music. 1,929,030. October 3, 1933.

Apparatus for the production of music. 1,929,031. October 3, 1933.

Apparatus for the production of music. 1,929,032. October 3, 1933. [With C. T. Jacobs.]

Method and apparatus for the production of music. 1,933,295. October 31, 1933.

Method and apparatus for the production of music. 1,933,297. October 31, 1933.

Method and apparatus for the production of music. 1,933,298. October 31, 1933.

Amplifier energizing. 1,940,723. December 26, 1933.

Push-pull amplifier system. 1,946,092. February 6, 1934.

Electrical filter system. 1,947,218. February 13, 1934.

Electrical rectifying and filtering system. 1,948,307. February 20, 1934.

Electrical amplifying system. 1,958,062. May 8, 1934.

Amplifying and reproducing system. 1,958,198. May 8, 1934.

Amplifying system. 1,963,668. June 19, 1934. [With C. T. Jacobs.]

Method and apparatus for the production of music. 1,961,159. June 5, 1934.

Method and apparatus for the production of music. 1,977,832. October 23, 1934.

Apparatus for the production of music. 1,979,633. November 6, 1934.

Amplifier system. 1,983,802. December 11, 1934.

Electrical rectifying and filtering system. 1,984,418. December 18, 1934.

Electric amplifying system. 1,985,945. January 1, 1935.

Amplifying and reproducing system. 1,985,946. January 1, 1935.

Method and apparatus for the production of music. 1,992,438. February 26, 1935.

System for energizing space discharge devices. 2,001,148. May 14, 1935.

Apparatus for the production of music. 2,001,391. May 14, 1935.

Method and apparatus for the production of music. 2,001,392. May 14, 1935.

Electromagnetic translating system. 2,002,919. May 28, 1935.

Apparatus for the production of music. 2,007,302. July 9, 1935.

Amplifier system. 2,027,054. January 7, 1936.

Apparatus for the production of music. 2,027,074. January 7, 1936.

Apparatus for the production of music. 2,033,440. March 10, 1936.

Multiple electrode discharge tube energizing. 2,034,663. March 17, 1936.

Method and apparatus for the production of music. 2,045,917. June 30, 1936.

Alarm system. 2,071,933. February 23, 1937.

Apparatus for the production of music. 2,071,649. February 23, 1937. [With C. T. Jacobs.]

Amplifying and reproducing system. 2,107,125. February 1, 1938.

Apparatus for the production of music. 2,138,500. November 29, 1938.

Method and apparatus for the production of music. 2,140,025. December 13, 1938.

Apparatus for the production of music. 2,168,623. August 8, 1939.

Apparatus for the production of music. Reissue 21,225. October 3, 1939. [With C. T. Jacobs.]

Method and apparatus for the production of music. 2,187,611. January 16, 1940.

Method and apparatus for the production of music. 2,187,612. January 16, 1940.

Electronic piano. 2,200,718. May 14, 1940.

Apparatus for the production of music. 2,215,708. September 24, 1940.

Apparatus for the production of music. 2,215,709. September 24, 1940.

Apparatus for the production of music. 2,225,195. December 17, 1940.

Electronic orchestra monitoring system. 2,225,196. December 17, 1940.

Apparatus for the production of music. 2,233,058. February 25, 1941.

Apparatus for the production of music. 2,237,105. April 1, 1941.

Apparatus for the production of music. 2,246,855. June 24, 1941.

Apparatus for the production of music. 2,271,460. January 27, 1942.

Apparatus for the production of music. 2,273,975. February 24, 1942.

Phonographic pickup device. 2,319,622. May 18, 1943.

Apparatus for the production of music. 2,323,232. June 29, 1943.

Tool for stringing tennis rackets. 2,352,730. July 4, 1944.

Apparatus for the production of music. 2,414,886. January 28, 1947.

Piano action. 2,469,568. May 10, 1949.

Vibrator-exciting action. 2,533,830. December 12, 1950.

Vibrator-exciting action. 2,535,503. December 26, 1950.

Apparatus for the production of music. 2,594,967. April 29, 1952.

Antileak fountain pen. 2,597,664. May 20, 1952.

Vibratory reed musical instrument. 2,640,384. June 2, 1953.

Antileak fountain pen. 2,642,041. June 16, 1953.

Fountain pen. 2,642,043. June 16, 1953.

Photoelectric translating system. 2,654,810. October 6, 1953.

Apparatus for the production of music. 2,656,755. October 27, 1953.

Antiflood fountain pen. 2,669,223. February 16, 1954.

Pen nib with spreader. 2,669,224. February 16, 1954.

Vibratory reed electronic musical instrument. 2,672,781. March 23, 1954.

Antiflooding fountain pen. 2,693,172. November 2, 1954.

Nonflooding fountain pen. 2,694,382. November 16, 1954.

Non-leaking fountain pen. 2,713,848. July 26, 1955.

Non-leaking and flooding pen. 2,724,366. November 22, 1955.

Radio frequency, electro-dynamic pick-up system. 2,704,957. March 29, 1955.

Implement for using fluid inks. 2,753,845. July 10, 1956.

Fountain pen with valve normally closing the air-and-ink tube. 2,753,846. July 10, 1956.

Vibratory reed. 2,755,697. July 24, 1956.

Electrical tone generator. 2,761,127. August 28, 1956.

Vibrator exciting action. 2,767,608. October 23, 1956.

Non-flooding fountain pen. 2,771,059. November 20, 1956.

Vibratory exciting action. 2,813,447. November 19, 1957.

Mounting arrangement for vibratory reeds. 2,826,109. March 11, 1958.

Sound reproducing device. 2,832,843. April 29, 1958.

Tone generators for electronic musical instruments. 2,834,243. May 13, 1958.

Key action for musical instrument. 2,845,829. August 5, 1958.

Clamping and control apparatus for reed generators used in electronic music instruments. 2,919,616. January 5, 1960.

Tone generating apparatus. 2,932,231. April 12, 1960.

Tuned reed. 2,934,988. May 3, 1960.

Electronic piano. 2,942,512. June 28, 1960.

Electronic piano. 2,966,821. January 3, 1961.

Tuned-vibrator musical instrument. 2,994,239. August 1, 1961.

Tone generator. 3,007,363. November 7, 1961.

Electronic piano. 3,038,363. June 12, 1962.

Electronic piano. 3,041,909. July 3, 1962.

Electrical pick-up for a reed musical instrument. 3,077,137. February 12, 1963.

Tone generating means for electrical musical instruments. 3,183,296. May 11, 1965.

Fountain pen. 3,183,893. May 18, 1965.

Alarm system. 3,184,727. May 18, 1965.

Electronic piano with improved inter-partial-ratio integralizing arrangements. 3,215,765. November 2, 1965.

Fixed-free-reed electronic piano with electrodynamic translating means controlling the odd and even partial-frequency components. 3,215,766. November 2, 1965.

Title Index

Alarm system. 2,071,933; 3,184,727.
Amplifier energizing. 1,940,723.
Amplifier energizing system. 1,842,558.
Amplifier system. 1,854,854; 1,963,668; 1,983,802; 2,027,054.
Amplifying and reproducing system. 1,958,198; 1,985,946; 2,107,125.
Antiflood fountain pen. 2,669,223.
Antiflooding fountain pen. 2,693,172.
Antileak fountain pen. 2,597,664; 2,642,041.
Apparatus for the production of music. 1,929,029; 1,929,030; 1,929,031; 1,929,032; 1,979,633; 2,001,391; 2,007,302; 2,027,074; 2,033,440; 2,071,649; 2,138,500; 2,168,623; 2,215,708; 2,215,709; 2,225,195; 2,233,058; 2,237,105; 2,246,855; 2,271,460; 2,273,975; 2,323,232; 2,414,886; 2,594,967; 2,656,755.
Apparatus for the production of music. Reissue 21,225. October 3, 1939.
"Cat's whisker." *See* 1,104,065.
Clamping and control apparatus for reed generators used in electronic music instruments. 2,919,616.
Detector for wireless apparatus. 1,104,065.
Discharge tube cathode energizing. 1,917,728.
Electric amplifying system. 1,985,945.
Electric music-chart. 1,268,376.
Electrical amplifier system. 1,790,874.
Electrical amplifying system. 1,834,414; 1,958,062.
Electrical filter system. 1,852,125; 1,853,217; 1,927,689; 1,947,218.

Electrical pick-up for a reed musical instrument. 3,077,137.
Electrical rectifying and filtering system. 1,948,307;
   1,984,418.
Electrical signal amplifying and repeating system. 1,719,189;
   1,789,950.
Electrical signal-amplifying system. 1,720,914.
Electrical supply and filter system. 1,788,342.
Electrical supply system. 1,912,991.
Electrical tone generator. 2,761,127.
Electrodynamic sound-reproducing system. 1,733,232.
Electromagnetic sound reproducer. 1,830,401; 1,830,402.
Electromagnetic translating device. 1,728,278; 2,002,919.
Electron discharge apparatus. 1,834,131.
Electron-discharge device. 1,718,059.
Electron tube. 1,859,454; 1,859,522; 1,890,911.
Electron tube energizing method and apparatus. 1,806,813.
Electronic orchestra monitoring system. 2,225,196.
Electronic piano. 2,200,718; 2,942,512; 2,966,821;
   3,038,363; 3,041,909.
Electronic piano with improved inter-partial-ratio integralizing
   arrangements. 3,215,765.
Electronic telephone. 1,593,636.
Fixed-free-reed electronic piano with electrodynamic
   translating means controlling the odd and even partial-
   frequency components. 3,215,766.
Fountain pen. 2,642,043; 3,183,893.
Fountain pen with valve normally closing the air-and-ink tube.
   2,753,846.
Implement for using fluid inks. 2,753,845.
Key action for musical instrument. 2,845,829.
Method and apparatus for the production of music. 1,912,293;
   1,915,858; 1,915,859, 1,915,860; 1,929,027; 1,929,028;
   1,933,295; 1,933,297; 1,933,298; 1,961,159; 1,977,832;
   1,992,438; 2,001,392, 2,045,917; 2,140,025; 2,187,611;
   2,187,612.
Method of and apparatus for changing voltage. 1,823,837.

Microphone. 1,722,851.

Mounting arrangement for vibratory reeds. 2,826,109.

Multiple electrode discharge tube energizing. 2,034,663.

Musical instrument. 1,698,958.

Non-flooding fountain pen. 2,694,382; 2,771,059.

Non-leaking and flooding pen. 2,724,366.

Non-leaking fountain pen. 2,713,848.

Pen nib with spreader. 2,669,224.

Phonographic pickup device. 2,319,622.

Photoelectric translating system. 2,654,810.

Piano action. 2,469,568.

Push-pull amplifier system. 1,946,092.

Radio communication device. 1,622,389.

Radio frequency, electro-dynamic pick-up system. 2,704,957.

Radio receiving system. 1,842,977.

Signal-lamp mounting. 1,729,080.

Sound amplifier. Design 64,507; 64,508. April 22, 1924.

Sound amplifying device. 1,639,048.

Sound reproducing device. 2,832,843.

Speaking-tube apparatus for aircraft. 1,418,388.

System for energizing space discharge devices. 2,001,148.

Telephone transmitter. 1,507,081.

Tone generating apparatus. 2,932,231.

Tone generating means for electrical musical instruments.
    3,183,296.

Tone generator. 3,007,363.

Tone generators for electronic musical instruments. 2,834,243.

Tool for stringing tennis rackets. 2,352,730.

Tuned reed. 2,934,988.

Tuned-vibrator musical instrument. 2,994,239.

Unidirectional current system. 1,832,646.

Vibrator-exciting action. 2,533,830; 2,535,503; 2,767,608.

Vibratory exciting action. 2,813,447.

Vibratory reed. 2,755,697.

Vibratory reed electronic musical instrument. 2,672,781.

Vibratory reed musical instrument. 2,640,384.

JOSEPH MURGAS (1864-1929)

Wireless-telegraph apparatus. 759,825. May 10, 1904. 110:582.

Communicating intelligence by wireless telegraphy. 759,826. May 10, 1904. 110:583.

Wave-meter. 848,675. April 2, 1907. 127:1612.

Electric transformer. 848,676. April 2, 1907. 127:1612.

Constructing antennae of wireless telegraphy. 860,051. July 16, 1907. 129:953.

Means for producing electromagnetic waves. 876,383. January 14, 1908. 132:260.

Wireless telegraphy. 915,993. March 23, 1909. 140:848.

Wireless telegraphy. 917,103. April 6, 1909. 141:52.

Magnetic-wave detector. 917,104. April 6, 1909. 141:52.

Electric-arc lamp. 923,127. May 25, 1909. 142:1084. [L. O. Kozar, assignor of one-half to J. Murgas.]

Magnetic detector. 930,780. August 10, 1909. 145:411.

Carbon-feeding mechanism for arc-lamps. 945,960. January 11, 1910. 150:354. [Ladislaw O. Kozar, assignor of one-third to J. Murgas.]

Apparatus for producing electric oscillations. 1,001,975. August 29, 1911. 169:1078.

Casting-reel. 1,024,739. April 30, 1912. 177:1139.

Method of and apparatus for producing electric oscillations from alternating currents. 1,196,969. September 5, 1916. 230:82.

Title Index

GREENLEAF W. PICKARD (1877-1956)

Wave-detecting device. 707,266. August 19, 1902. 100:1645. [With H. Shoemaker.]

Coherer. 708,070. September 2, 1902. 100:2008.

Wireless-telegraph system. 708,071. September 2, 1902. 100:2008.

Wireless telegraphy. 708,072. September 2, 1902. 100:2008.

Wireless signaling system. 711,174. October 14, 1902. 101:327.

Wireless signaling system. 717,765. January 6, 1903. 102:100. [With H. Shoemaker.]

Alternating-current relay. 749,399. January 12, 1904. 108:414.

Alternating-current signal-receiving apparatus. 758,468. April 26, 1904. 109:2366.

Signal system for electric railways. 786,148. March 28, 1905. 115:1011.

Apparatus for electrostatic separation. 796,011. August 1, 1905. 117:1270.

Electrostatic separation. 796,012. August 1, 1905. 117:1271.

Carbon plate for protective devices. 807,962. December 19, 1905. 119:2160.

Protective device. 807,963. December 19, 1905. 119:2160.

Electrostatic separation. 827,115. July 31, 1906. 123:1311.

Apparatus for electrostatic separation. 827,116. July 31, 1906. 123:1311.

Means for receiving intelligence communicated by electric waves. 836,531. November 20, 1906. 125:898.

Electrostatic separator. 840,802. January 8, 1907. 126:561.

Wireless communication. 842,910. February 5, 1907. 126:1825.

Means for receiving intelligence communicated by electric waves. 845,316. February 26, 1907. 126:561.

Intelligence intercommunication by magnetic-wave components. 876,996. January 21, 1908. 132:506.

Means for receiving intelligence communicated by electric waves. 877,451. January 21, 1908. 132:657.

Oscillation-receiver. 886,154. April 28, 1908. 133:2090.

Oscillation-receiver. 888,191. May 19, 1908. 134:666.

Electrical condenser. 893,811. July 21, 1908. 135:530.

Oscillation-detecting means for receiving intelligence communicated by electric waves. 904,222. November 17, 1908. 137:620.

Oscillation detector and rectifier. 912,613. February 16, 1909. 139:590.

Oscillation-receiver. 912,726. February 16, 1909. 139:620.

Oscillation-receiver. 924,827. June 15, 1909. 143:637.

Oscillation device. 933,263. September 7, 1909. 146:82.

Electrical space communication. 956,165. April 26, 1910. 153:943.

Oscillation-receiver. 963,173. July 5, 1910. 156:52.

Telephone receiving apparatus. 972,715. October 11, 1910. 159:446.

Meter for electromagnetic-wave communication. 993,316. May 23, 1911. 166:952.

Amplifier. 1,027,755. May 28, 1912. 178:1012.

Electrical conduction system for communicating electrical energy. 1,051,443. January 28, 1913. 186:827.

Detector for wireless telegraphy and telephony. 1,104,073. July 21, 1914. 204:731.

Means for receiving intelligence communicated by electrical waves. Reissue 13,798. September 8, 1914. 206:558.

Oscillation-detector. 1,118,228. November 24, 1914. 208:1081.

Apparatus for radio communication. 1,127,921. February 9, 1915. 211:481.

Valve-detector for wireless. 1,128,817. February 16, 1915. 211:842.

Oscillation-receiving device. 1,136,044. April 20, 1915. 213:777.

Oscillation-receiving device. 1,136,045. April 20, 1915. 213:777.

Oscillation-receiving device. 1,136,046. April 20, 1915. 213:777.

Oscillation-receiving device. 1,136,047. April 20, 1915. 213:777.

Solid rectifier for feeble electric currents. 1,137,714. April 27, 1915. 213:1403.

Radio telegraphy and telephony receiver. 1,144,969. June 29, 1915. 215:1482.

Wireless receiving improvement. 1,156,625. October 12, 1915. 219:478.

Apparatus for radio communication. 1,176,925. March 28, 1916. 224:1132.

Radio telegraphy and telephony receiver. 1,184,376. May 23, 1916. 226:1279.

Receiver for wireless telegraphy and telephony. 1,185,711. June 6, 1916. 227:40.

System of radio communication. 1,206,911. December 5, 1916. 233:43.

Means for receiving intelligence communicated by electric waves. 1,213,250. January 23, 1917. 234:1093.

Radio telegraphy and telephony receiver. 1,224,499. May 1, 1917. 238:137.

Rectifier. 1,225,852. May 15, 1917. 238:693.

Radio telegraphy and telephony receiver. 1,245,266. November 6, 1917. 244:37.

Radio telegraphy and telephony receiver. 1,245,267. November 6, 1917. 244:37.

Radio telegraphy and telephony receiver. 1,249,482. December 11, 1917. 245:335.

Constant-pressure solid rectifier. 1,257,526. February 26, 1918. 247:818.

Apparatus for measuring telephone-currents. 1,324,465. December 9, 1919. 269:280.

Interference preventer. 1,460,439. July 3, 1923.

Reed telephone receiving. 1,472,341. October 30, 1923.

Electromagnetic compass. 1,472,342. October 30, 1923.

Optical selection of split mica sheets. 1,476,102. December 4, 1923.

Electrical condenser and making the same. 1,479,315. January 1, 1924.

Protective means for condenser installations. 1,483,552. February 12, 1924.

Vacuous electrical apparatus. 1,488,613. April 1, 1924.

Electrical condenser. 1,503,765. August 5, 1924.

Process and apparatus for the manufacture of electrical condensers. 1,505,600. August 19, 1924.

Vernier for tuning reactances. 1,536,453. May 5, 1925.

Industrial composition and process. 1,547,666. July 28, 1925.

Testing apparatus. 1,555,249. September 29, 1925.

Distinguishing dielectric sheets. 1,561,483. November 17, 1925.

Closed tuned coil or loop aerial. 1,567,542. December 29, 1925.

Thermionic tube. 1,650,232. November 22, 1927.

Electrical condenser. 1,655,022. January 3, 1928.

Electrical amplifier. 1,676,744. July 10, 1928.

Electrical reactance and method and apparatus. 1,676,745. July 10, 1928.

Closed tuned coil or loop aerial. 1,679,095. July 31, 1928.

High-tension electrical condenser. 1,696,895. December 25, 1928.

Electrical condenser and process. 1,706,816. March 26, 1929.

Radio apparatus. 1,708,453. April 9, 1929.

Radio apparatus. 1,718,431. June 25, 1929.

Phonographic machine. 1,744,838. January 28, 1930.

Electrical condenser. 1,758,968. May 20, 1930.

Radio amplifying system. 1,770,143. July 8, 1930.

Electrical condenser. 1,841,628. January 19, 1932.

Universally adjustable radio apparatus for aircraft. 1,889,568. November 29, 1932.

Electrical condenser and making the same. 1,892,362. December 27, 1932.

Radio receiving apparatus. 1,907,571. May 9, 1933.

Static neutralizer for radioreceivers. 1,907,572. May 9, 1933.

Condenser support. 1,915,692. June 27, 1933.

Extreme loading condenser. 1,918,825. July 18, 1933.

Electrical condenser. 1,938,857. December 12, 1933.

Magnetic compass. 1,946,710. February 13, 1934.

Insulating casing condenser with horizontal stack. 1,994,533. March 19, 1935.

Directive receiver. 2,026,359. December 31, 1935.

Direction finding system. 2,155,838. April 25, 1939.

Title Index

Alternating-current relay. 749,399.
Alternating-current signal-receiving apparatus. 758,468.
Amplifier. 1,027,755.
Apparatus for electrostatic separation. 796,011; 827,116.
Apparatus for measuring telephone-currents. 1,324,465.
Apparatus for radio communication. 1,127,921; 1,176,925.
Carbon plate for protective devices. 807,962.
Closed tuned coil or loop aerial. 1,567,542; 1,679,095.
Coherer. 708,070.
Condenser support. 1,915,692.
Constant-pressure solid rectifier. 1,257,526.
Crystal detector. *See* 1,104,073.
Detector for wireless telegraphy and telephony. 1,104,073.
Direction finding system. 2,155,838.
Directive receiver. 2,026,359.
Distinguishing dielectric sheets. 1,561,483.
Electrical amplifier. 1,676,744.
Electrical condenser. 893,811; 1,503,765; 1,655,022;
    1,758,968; 1,841,628; 1,938,857.
Electrical condenser and making the same. 1,479,315;
    1,892,362.
Electrical condenser and process. 1,706,816.
Electrical conduction system for communicating electrical
    energy. 1,051,443.
Electrical reactance and method and apparatus. 1,676,745.
Electrical space communication. 956,165.
Electromagnetic compass. 1,472,342.
Electrostatic separation. 796,012; 827,115.
Electrostatic separator. 840,802.
Extreme loading condenser. 1,918,825.
High-tension electrical condenser. 1,696,895.

Industrial composition and process. 1,547,666.
Insulating casing condenser with horizontal stack. 1,994,533.
Intelligence intercommunication by magnetic-wave
    components. 876,996.
Interference preventer. 1,460,439.
Magnetic compass. 1,946,710.
Means for receiving intelligence communicated by electric
    waves. 836,531; 845,316; 877,451; 1,213,250.
Means for receiving intelligence communicated by electrical
    waves. Reissue 13,798. September 8, 1914.
Meter for electromagnetic-wave communication. 993,316.
Optical selection of split mica sheets. 1,476,102.
Oscillation device. 933,263.
Oscillation-detecting means for receiving intelligence
    communicated by electric waves. 904,222.
Oscillation-detector. 1,118,228.
Oscillation detector and rectifier. 912,613.
Oscillation-receiver. 886,154; 888,191; 912,726; 924,827;
    963,173.
Oscillation-receiving device. 1,136,044; 1,136,045;
    1,136,046; 1,136,047.
Phonographic machine. 1,744,838.
Process and apparatus for the manufacture of electrical
    condensers. 1,505,600.
Protective device. 807,963.
Protective means for condenser installations. 1,483,552.
Radio amplifying system. 1,770,143.
Radio apparatus. 1,708,453; 1,718,431.
Radio receiving apparatus. 1,907,571.
Radio telegraphy and telephony receiver. 1,144,969;
    1,184,376; 1,224,499; 1,245,266; 1,245,267; 1,249,482.
Receiver for wireless telegraphy and telephony. 1,185,711.
Rectifier. 1,225,852.
Reed telephone receiving. 1,472,341.
Signal system for electric railways. 786,148.
Solid rectifier for feeble electric currents. 1,137,714.

Static neutralizer for radioreceivers. 1,907,572.
System of radio communication. 1,206,911.
Telephone receiving apparatus. 972,715.
Testing apparatus. 1,555,249.
Thermionic tube. 1,650,232.
Universally adjustable radio apparatus for aircraft. 1,889,568.
Vacuous electrical apparatus. 1,488,613.
Valve-detector for wireless. 1,128,817.
Vernier for tuning reactances. 1,536,453.
Wave-detecting device. 707,266.
Wireless communication. 842,910.
Wireless receiving improvement. 1,156,625.
Wireless signaling system. 711,174; 717,765.
Wireless-telegraph system. 708,071.
Wireless telegraphy. 708,072.

MICHAEL I. PUPIN (1858-1935)

Apparatus for telegraphic or telephonic transmission. 519,346. May 8, 1894. 67:696.

Transformer for telegraphic, telephonic, or other electrical systems. 519,347. May 8, 1894. 67:697.

Distributing electrical energy by alternating currents. 640,515. January 2, 1900. 90:133.

Electrical transmission by resonance-circuits. 640,516. January 2, 1900. 90:134.

Reducing attenuation of electrical waves and apparatus therefor. 652,230. June 19, 1900. 91:2361.

Reducing attenuation of electrical waves. 652,231. June 19, 1900. 91:2362.

Winding-machine. 697,660. April 15, 1902. 99:535. [With S. W. Balch.]

Multiple telegraphy. 707,007. August 12, 1902. 100:1525.

Multiple telegraphy. 707,008. August 12, 1902. 100:1525.

Producing asymmetrical currents from symmetrical alternating electromotive forces. 713,044. November 4, 1902. 101:1116.

Apparatus for producing asymmetrical currents from symmetrical alternating electromotive forces. 713,045. November 4, 1902. 101:1116.

Apparatus for reducing attenuation of electrical waves. 761,995. June 7, 1904. 110:1602.

Wireless electrical signaling. 768,301. August 23, 1904. 111:2076.

Telegraphy. 821,741. May 29, 1906. 122:1465.

Electric-wave transmission. 1,334,165. March 16, 1920. 272:489. [With E. H. Armstrong.]

Antenna with distributed positive resistance. 1,336,378. April 6, 1920. 273:127.

Multiple antenna for electrical wave transmission. 1,388,441. August 23, 1921. 289:674. [With E. H. Armstrong.]

Sound-generator. 1,399,877. December 13, 1921.

Selectively opposing impedance to received electrical oscillations. 1,415,845. May 9, 1922. [With E. H. Armstrong.]

Radioreceiving system having high selectivity. 1,416,061. May 16, 1922. [With E. H. Armstrong.]

Aperiodic pilot conductor. 1,446,769. February 27, 1923. [With M. C. Spencer.]

Selective amplifying apparatus. 1,452,833. April 24, 1923.

Wave conductor. 1,456,909. May 29, 1923.

Selective amplifying apparatus. 1,488,514. January 1, 1924.

Electrical tuning. 1,494,803. May 20, 1924.

Tone-producing radioreceiver. 1,502,875. July 29, 1924.
[With E. H. Armstrong.]

Electrical wave transmission. 1,541,845. June 16, 1925.

Wave signaling system. 1,561,278. November 10, 1925.

Equalizing vacuum-tube amplifier. 1,561,279. November 10, 1925.

Electromagnetic production of direct current without fluctuations. 1,571,458. February 2, 1926.

Electrical pulse generator. 1,657,587. January 31, 1928.

Telegraph system. 1,811,368. June 23, 1931.

Inductive artificial line. 1,834,735. December 1, 1931.

Supply system for vacuum tubes. 1,983,774. December 11, 1934.

Title Index

Distributing electrical energy by alternating currents. 640,515.
Electric-wave transmission. 1,334,165.
Electrical pulse generator. 1,657,587.
Electrical transmission by resonance-circuits. 640,516.
Electrical tuning. 1,494,803.
Electrical wave transmission. 1,541,845.
Electromagnetic production of direct current without
    fluctuations. 1,571,458.
Equalizing vacuum-tube amplifier. 1,561,279.
Inductive artificial line. 1,834,735.
Multiple antenna for electrical wave transmission. 1,388,441.
Multiple telegraphy. 707,007; 707,008.
Producing asymmetrical currents from symmetrical alternating
    electromotive forces. 713,044.
Radioreceiving system having high selectivity. 1,416,061.
Reducing attenuation of electrical waves. 652,231.
Reducing attenuation of electrical waves and apparatus
    therefor. 652,230.
Selective amplifying apparatus. 1,452,833; 1,488,514.
Selectively opposing impedance to received electrical
    oscillations. 1,415,845.
Sound-generator. 1,399,877.
Supply system for vacuum tubes. 1,983,774.
Telegraph system. 1,811,368.
Telegraphy. 821,741.
Tone-producing radioreceiver. 1,502,875.
Transformer for telegraphic, telephonic, or other electrical
    systems. 519,347.
Wave conductor. 1,456,909.
Wave signaling system. 1,561,278.
Winding-machine. 697,660.
Wireless electrical signaling. 768,301.

JOHN F. RIDER (1900-1985)

Switching device for radio receiving and other electrical systems. 2,064,348. December 15, 1936. [With Paul Kalencik.]

Measurement of electrical constants of tuned circuits. 2,111,235. March 15, 1938. [With Jack Avins.]

Electrical testing system. 2,227,381. December 31, 1940. [With Jack Avins.]

Multisection book. 2,308,628. January 19, 1943.

Oscillator for sine waves and square waves. 2,346,396. April 11, 1944.

Unitary volume-control switch and dialite assembly. 2,457,920. January 4, 1949.

Single button tuning control for radio sets. 2,487,760. November 8, 1949. [With Richard F. Koch.]

Composite test probe for radio apparatus and the like. 2,488,328. November 15, 1949.

DAVID SARNOFF (1891-1971)

Secret radio signaling system. 2,455,443. December 7, 1948.

Early warning relay system. 2,571,386. October 16, 1951.

MCMURDO SILVER (1903-1948)

Radio receiver. 2,062,379. December 1, 1936.

JOHN S. STONE (1869-1943)

Electric cable. 469,475. February 23, 1892. 58:1029. [With Hammond V. Hayes.]

Development and distribution of electricity. 487,102. November 29, 1892. 61:1262.

Telephone-circuit. 507,568. October 31, 1893. 65:621.

Telephone-transmitter circuit and apparatus. 507,694. October 31, 1893. 65:661.

Telephone-circuit. 508,255. November 7, 1893. 65:842.

Telephonic transmission. 509,965. December 5, 1893. 65:1446.

Telephone circuit. 551,060. December 10, 1895. 73:1596.

Telephone circuit. 553,179. January 14, 1896. 74:251. [With Edward Slade.]

Telephone speaking-tube system. 556,034. March 10, 1896. 74:1328.

Telephone circuit. 560,761. May 26, 1896. 75:1247.

Telephone circuit and apparatus. 560,762. May 26, 1896. 75:1248.

System of current supply for telephone-circuits. 562,435. June 23, 1896. 75:1882.

Telephone signaling-circuit. 563,692. July 7, 1896. 76:144.

Resonant electric circuit. 577,214. February 16, 1897. 78:1032.

Electric circuit. 578,275. March 2, 1897. 78:1408.

Telephone circuit. 580,166. April 6, 1897. 79:87.

Telephone repeater or relay. 609,374. August 16, 1898. 84:1121.

Differential electromagnet. 623,579. April 25, 1899. 87:547.

Telephony. 638,152. November 28, 1899. 89:1825.

Selective electric signaling. 714,756. December 2, 1902. 101:1878. [Assignor to L. E. Whicher, A. P. Browne, and B. T. Judkins, trustees.]

Apparatus for selective electric signaling. 714,831. December 2, 1902. 101:1906. [Assignor to L. E. Whicher, A. P. Browne, and B. T. Judkins, trustees.]

Apparatus for amplifying electromagnetic signal-waves. 714,832. December 2, 1902. 101:1910. [Assignor to L. E. Whicher, A. P. Browne, and B. T. Judkins, trustees.]

Amplifying electromagnetic signal-waves. 714,833. December 2, 1902. 101:1910. [Assignor to L. E. Whicher, A. P. Browne, and B. T. Judkins, trustees.]

Apparatus for selective electric signaling. 714,834. December
2, 1902. 101:1910. [Assignor to L. E. Whicher, A. P.
Browne, and B. T. Judkins, trustees.]

Determining the direction of space-telegraph signals. 716,134.
December 16, 1902. 101:2470. [Assignor to L. E. Whicher,
A. P. Browne, and B. T. Judkins, trustees.]

Apparatus for determining the direction of space-telegraph
signals. 716,135. December 16, 1902. 101:2470. [Assignor to
L. E. Whicher, A. P. Browne, and B. T. Judkins, trustees.]

Apparatus for simultaneously transmitting and receiving space-
telegraph signals. 716,136. December 16, 1902. 101:2470.
[Assignor to L. E. Whicher, A. P. Browne, and B. T.
Judkins, trustees.]

Simultaneously transmitting and receiving space-telegraph
signals. 716,137. December 16, 1902. 101:2470. [Assignor to
L. E. Whicher, A. P. Browne, and B. T. Judkins, trustees.]

Simultaneously transmitting and receiving space-telegraph
signals. 716,955. December 30, 1902. 101:2870. [Assignor to
L. E. Whicher, A. P. Browne, and B. T. Judkins, trustees.]

Electrical distribution. 717,467. December 30, 1902.
101:3073.

Apparatus for relaying space-telegraph signals. 717,509.
December 30, 1902. 101:3089. [Assignor to L. E. Whicher,
A. P. Browne, and B. T. Judkins, trustees.]

Relaying space-telegraph signals. 717,510. December 30,
1902. 101:3089. [Assignor to L. E. Whicher, A. P. Browne,
and B. T. Judkins, trustees.]

Tuning vertical wire oscillators. 717,511. December 30, 1902. 101:3089. [Assignor to L. E. Whicher, A. P. Browne, and B. T. Judkins, trustees.]

Tuned electric oscillator. 717,512. December 30, 1902. 101:3089. [Assignor to L. E. Whicher, A. P. Browne, and B. T. Judkins, trustees.]

Relaying space-telegraph signals. 717,513. December 30, 1902. 101:3090. [Assignor to L. E. Whicher, A. P. Browne, and B. T. Judkins, trustees.]

Apparatus for relaying space-telegraph signals. 717,514. December 30, 1902. 101:3090. [Assignor to L. E. Whicher, A. P. Browne, and B. T. Judkins, trustees.]

Electrical distribution. 717,515. December 30, 1902. 101:3090.

Wireless or space telegraphy. 725,634. April 14, 1903. 103:1664.

Space telegraphy. 725,635. April 14, 1903. 103:1665.

Space telegraphy. 725,636. April 14, 1903. 103:1666.

Electrical distribution and selective distribution. 726,368. April 28, 1903. 103:1976

Electrical distribution and selective distribution. 726,476. April 28, 1903. 103:2016.

Electrical distribution and selective distribution. 729,103. May 26, 1903. 104:956.

Electrical apparatus and circuits for electrical distribution and selective distribution. 729,104. May 26, 1903. 104:957.

Apparatus for selective electric signaling. Reissue 12,141. August 4, 1903. 105:1249.

Apparatus for selective electric signaling. 737,170. August 25, 1903. 105:1880.

Determining the direction of space-telegraph signals. Reissue 12,148. August 18, 1903. 105:1766.

Apparatus for selective electrical signaling. Reissue 12,149. August 25, 1903. 105:2044.

Apparatus for amplifying electromagnetic signal-waves. Reissue 12,151. September 8, 1903. 106:530.

Amplifying electromagnetic signal-waves. Reissue 12,152. September 8, 1903. 106:530.

Apparatus for simultaneously transmitting and receiving space-telegraph signals. 767,970. August 16, 1904. 111:1891.

Wireless-telegraph receiving device. 767,971. August 16, 1904. 111:1893.

Receiving space-telegraph signals. 767,972. August 16, 1904. 111:1895.

Increasing the effective radiation of electromagnetic waves. 767,973. August 16, 1904. 111:1896. [With W. W. Swan, trustee.]

Apparatus for increasing the effective radiation of electromagnetic waves. 767,974. August 16, 1904. 111:1897. [With W. W. Swan, trustee.]

Space telegraphy. 767,975 through 768,005. August 16, 1904. 111:1897 through 1918. [All with W. W. Swan, trustee.]

Protecting telephone-circuits from the action of electromagnetic waves. 781,625. January 31, 1905. 114:1250.

Space telegraphy. 802,417 through 802,432. October 24, 1905. 118:1962 through 1970. [W. W. Swan, trustee.]

Space telephony. 803,199. October 31, 1905. 118:2353.

Space telephony. 803,513. October 31, 1905. 118:2485.

Device for amplifying electrical currents. 854,120. May 21, 1907. 128:981.

Space telegraphy. 864,272. August 27, 1907. 129:3227.

Space telegraphy. 884,106 through 884,109. April 7, 1908. 133:1334 through 1335. [Assignor to W. W. Swan, trustee.]

Space telegraphy. 884,110. April 7, 1908. 133:1336. [With S. Cabot; assignors to W. W. Swan, trustee.]

Apparatus for determining the direction of space-telegraph signals. 899,272. September 22, 1908. 136:748. [Assignor to W. W. Swan, trustee.]

Condenser. 908,814. January 5, 1909. 138:125.

Space telegraphy. 908,815. January 5, 1909. 138:125.

Space telegraphy. 916,895. March 30, 1909. 140:1166.

Space telegraphy. 946,166 through 946,168. January 11, 1910. 150:424.

Apparatus for determining the direction of space-telegraph signals. 961,265. June 14, 1910. 155:373.

Space telegraphy. 986,651. March 14, 1911. 164:336.

Resistance amplifier. 1,555,037. September 29, 1925.

Secret-communication system. 1,565,521. December 15, 1925. [With C. C. Rose.]

Carrier-current multiplex signaling system. 1,565,522. December 15, 1925.

Radio transmitting system. 1,567,204. December 29, 1925.

Thermionic modulator. 1,573,282. February 16, 1926.

Amplifier. 1,590,263. June 29, 1926.

Multiplex radio telegraphy and telephony. 1,598,663. September 7, 1926.

Signaling system. 1,605,010. November 2, 1926.

Circuits for passing or stopping a frequency band of alternating currents. 1,610,336. December 14, 1926.

Directive antenna array. 1,643,323. September 27, 1927.

Reactance neutralizing network. 1,674,705. June 26, 1928.

Directive antenna array. 1,683,739. September 11, 1928.

Antenna array. 1,715,433. June 4, 1929.

Associated resonant circuits. 1,720,770. July 16, 1929.

Radio receiving system. 1,789,419. January 20, 1931.

Directional antenna array. 1,808,867. June 9, 1931.

Directional antenna array. 1,808,868. June 9, 1931.

Directional antenna array. 1,808,869. June 9, 1931.

Advertising device. 1,822,511. September 8, 1931. [With G. Wilson.]

Valve commutator and its use in multiplex signaling. 1,835,099. December 8, 1931.

Time switch. 1,893,904. January 10, 1933. [With John B. Petrus.]

Apparatus and method for radio transmission and reception. 1,919,309. June 25, 1933.

Antenna array. 1,922,115. August 15, 1933.

Antenna array. 1,922,116. August 15, 1933.

Sound amplifier. 1,929,569. October 10, 1933.

Radioantenna. 1,941,636. January 2, 1934.

Radio receiving system. 1,954,898. April 17, 1934.

Reenforced soap cake. 1,997,474. April 9, 1935.

Frequency selective communication system. 2,023,556. December 10, 1935.

Composite oscillator for electromagnetic waves. 2,026,712. January 7, 1936.

Radio receiving system. 2,037,154. April 14, 1936.

Condenser telephone transmitter circuit. 2,232,891. February 25, 1941.

Frequency sensitive elements. 2,301,828. November 10, 1942.

Title Index

Apparatus for selective electric signaling. 714,831; 714,834; 737,170.

Apparatus for selective electric signaling. Reissue 12,141. August 4, 1903.

Apparatus for selective electrical signaling. Reissue 12,149. August 25, 1903.

Apparatus for simultaneously transmitting and receiving space-telegraph signals. 716,136; 767,970.

Associated resonant circuits. 1,720,770.

Carrier-current multiplex signaling system. 1,565,522.

Circuits for passing or stopping a frequency band of alternating currents. 1,610,336.

Composite oscillator for electromagnetic waves. 2,026,712.

Condenser. 908,814.

Condenser telephone transmitter circuit. 2,232,891.

Determining the direction of space-telegraph signals. 716,134.

Determining the direction of space-telegraph signals. Reissue 12,148. August 18, 1903.

Development and distribution of electricity. 487,102.

Device for amplifying electrical currents. 854,120.

Differential electromagnet. 623,579.

Directional antenna array. 1,808,867; 1,808,868; 1,808,869.

Directive antenna array. 1,643,323; 1,683,739.

Electric cable. 469,475.

Electric circuit. 578,275.

Electrical apparatus and circuits for electrical distribution and selective distribution. 729,104.

Electrical distribution. 717,467; 717,515.

Electrical distribution and selective distribution. 726,368; 726,476; 729,103.

Frequency selective communication system. 2,023,556.

Frequency sensitive elements. 2,301,828.

Increasing the effective radiation of electromagnetic waves. 767,973.

Multiplex radio telegraphy and telephony. 1,598,663.

Protecting telephone-circuits from the action of
  electromagnetic waves. 781,625.
Radio receiving system. 1,789,419; 1,954,898; 2,037,154.
Radio transmitting system. 1,567,204.
Radioantenna. 1,941,636.
Reactance neutralizing network. 1,674,705.
Receiving space-telegraph signals. 767,972.
Reenforced soap cake. 1,997,474.
Relaying space-telegraph signals. 717,510; 717,513.
Resistance amplifier. 1,555,037.
Resonant electric circuit. 577,214.
Secret-communication system. 1,565,521.
Selective electric signaling. 714,756.
Signaling system. 1,605,010.
Simultaneously transmitting and receiving space-telegraph
  signals. 716,137; 716,955.
Sound amplifier. 1,929,569.
Space telegraphy. 725,635; 725,636; 767,975 through
  768,005; 802,417 through 802,432; 864,272; 884,106;
  884,110; 908,815; 916,895; 946,166 through 946,168;
  986,651.
Space telephony. 803,199; 803,513.
System of current supply for telephone-circuits. 562,435.
Telephone circuit. 507,568; 508,255; 551,060; 553,179;
  560,761; 580,166.
Telephone circuit and apparatus. 560,762.
Telephone repeater or relay. 609,374.
Telephone signaling-circuit. 563,692.
Telephone speaking-tube system. 556,034.
Telephone-transmitter circuit and apparatus. 507,694.
Telephonic transmission. 509,965.
Telephony. 638,152.
Thermionic modulator. 1,573,282.
Time switch. 1,893,904.
Tuned electric oscillator. 717,512.
Tuning vertical wire oscillators. 717,511.

Valve commutator and its use in multiplex signaling.
1,835,099.
Wireless or space telegraphy. 725,634.
Wireless-telegraph receiving device. 767,971.

NATHAN B. STUBBLEFIELD (1860?-1928)

Lighting device. 329,864. November 3, 1885. 33:616.

Mechanical telephone. 378,183. February 21, 1888. 42:758.
[With S. C. Holcomb.]

Electrical battery. 600,457. March 8, 1898. 82:1528. [With
W. G. Love.]

Wireless telephone. 887,357. May 12, 1908. 134:365.
[Assignor of twelve and one-half one-hundredths to C. Linn,
five one-hundredths to R. Downs, five one-hundredths to
B. F. Schroader, five one-hundredths to G. C. McLarin, five
one-hundredths to J. P. McElrath, two and one-half one-
hundredths to J. D. Roulett, and one-twentieth to S. E.
Bynum, Murray, Ky.]

SARKES TARZIAN (1900-1987)

[Note: Patents assigned to Sarkes Tarzian, Inc., but not in Tarzian's name are not listed.]

Volume control. 1,755,310. April 22, 1930.

Radio receiving apparatus. 1,814,744. July 14, 1931.

Radio receiving apparatus. 1,867,037. July 12, 1932.

Volume control. 1,885,307. November 1, 1932.

Anode supply system. 1,972,279. September 4, 1934. [With A. Atwater Kent.]

Radio apparatus. 1,973,293. September 11, 1934. [With John M. Miller.]

Volume control. 1,978,514. October 30, 1934.

Radio tuning apparatus. 2,001,076. May 14, 1935.

Variable high frequency transformer. 2,181,982. December 5, 1939.

Frequency modulation converter system. 2,528,187. October 31, 1950. [With George C. Sziklai.]

Selenium and like rectifier stack. 2,620,384. December 2, 1952.

Television channel selecting apparatus. 3,247,437. April 19,
1966. [With Stanley R. Meadows.]

Title Index

Anode supply system. 1,972,279.
Frequency modulation converter system. 2,528,187.
Radio apparatus. 1,973,293.
Radio receiving apparatus. 1,814,744; 1,867,037.
Radio tuning apparatus. 2,001,076.
Selenium and like rectifier stack. 2,620,384.
Television channel selecting apparatus. 3,247,437.
Variable high frequency transformer. 2,181,982.
Volume control. 1,755,310; 1,885,307; 1,978,514.

CLARENCE TUSKA (1896-1985)

[Note: Patents assigned to the C. D. Tuska Company but not in Tuska's name are not listed.]

Condenser. 1,371,061. March 8, 1921. 284:293.

Condenser. 1,468,653. September 25, 1923.

Condenser. Reissue 15,689. September 25, 1923.

Pantograph engraving tool. 1,516,897. November 25, 1924. [With P. H. Spencer.]

Variocoupler. 1,523,464. January 20, 1925.

Variometer coil and making same. 1,525,836. February 19, 1925.

Dial knob. 1,527,617. February 24, 1925.

Variable condenser. 1,609,006. November 30, 1926.

Variometer. 1,630,873. May 31, 1927.

Mold for variometer. 1,630,874. May 31, 1927.

Binding post. 1,646,890. October 25, 1927.

Condenser. 1,708,110. April 9, 1929.

Condenser. 1,708,527. April 9, 1929.

Variable-capacity apparatus. 1,737,277. November 26, 1929.

Radio-cabinet. 1,746,750. February 11, 1930.

Radio circuit receiving system. 1,925,291. September 5, 1933.

Refrigeration system. 2,042,568. June 2, 1936.

Directional receiver. 2,279,021. April 7, 1942. [With P. G. Cooper.]

Ticket issuing machine. 2,400,793. May 21, 1946.

Obstacle detecting system. 2,403,622. July 9, 1946.

Bolt anchoring devices for concrete. 3,599,379. August 17, 1971. [With A. N. Spanel.]

Title Index

Binding post. 1,646,890.
Bolt anchoring devices for concrete. 3,599,379.
Condenser. 1,371,061; 1,468,653; 1,708,110; 1,708,527.
Condenser. Reissue 15,689. September 25, 1923.
Dial knob. 1,527,617.
Directional receiver. 2,279,021.
Mold for variometer. 1,630,874.
Obstacle detecting system. 2,403,622.
Pantograph engraving tool. 1,516,897.
Radio-cabinet. 1,746,750.
Radio circuit receiving system. 1,925,291.
Refrigeration system. 2,042,568.
Ticket issuing machine. 2,400,793.

Variable-capacity apparatus. 1,737,277.
Variable condenser. 1,609,006.
Variocoupler. 1,523,464.
Variometer. 1,630,873.
Variometer coil and making same. 1,525,836.

JOHN VICTOREEN (1902-1986)

[Note: Patents assigned to Victoreen, Inc., or Victoreen Instrument Company but not in Victoreen's name are not listed.]

Radiofrequency apparatus. 1,589,308. June 15, 1926.

Coil and making same. 1,674,934. June 26, 1928.

Audio frequency transformer. 1,703,912. March 5, 1929.

Master control. 1,735,363. November 12, 1929.

Illuminating device. 2,101,289. December 7, 1937.

Potential measuring apparatus. 2,162,412. June 13, 1939.

X-ray measuring instrument. 2,190,200. February 13, 1940.

Potential measuring apparatus. 2,235,268. March 18, 1942.

Electrical apparatus. 2,314,060. March 16, 1943.

Resistor and making the same. 2,416,599. February 25, 1947.

Method and apparatus for regulating water temperature. 2,456,094. December 14, 1948.

Vacuum tube with filamentary cathode. 2,462,441. February 22, 1949.

Recording or indicating. 2,507,743. May 16, 1950.

Geiger tube. 2,521,315. September 5, 1950.

Coin detecting and indicating apparatus. 2,540,063. January 30, 1951.

Geiger tube. 2,542,440. February 20, 1951. [With R. W. Barton.]

Ionization chamber. 2,573,999. November 6, 1951.

Ionization and vacuum tube chamber. 2,574,000. November 6, 1951.

Indicating pocket ionization chamber. 2,587,254. February 26, 1952.

Method and apparatus for photoelectrically assorting, recording, or computing. 2,600,817. June 17, 1952.

Electric battery and making same. 2,666,801. January 19, 1954.

Glow tube. 2,728,004. December 20, 1955. [With J. H. Eddleston.]

Gaseous discharge tube. 2,728,005. December 20, 1955.

Pocket ionization chamber. 2,756,346. July 24, 1956.

Apparatus for the comparison of sources of radiation. 2,876,360. March 3, 1959.

High fidelity sound translating apparatus. 2,989,597. June 20, 1961.

Method and apparatus for determining hearing characteristics. 3,073,900. January 15, 1963.

Transducer hearing aid coupling. 3,118,023. January 14, 1964.

Hearing aid transducer support. 3,172,963. March 9, 1965.

Method and apparatus for testing hearing. 3,408,460. October 29, 1968.

Sound reproducer. 3,478,840. November 18, 1969.

Hydraulically expandable earpiece. 3,602,654. August 31, 1971.

Audio oscillator for generating either C.W., damped wave trains, or narrow band noise. 3,652,953. March 28, 1972.

Audio oscillator for generating either C.W., damped wave trains, or narrow band noise. 3,755,755. August 28, 1973.

Condenser microphone having a plurality of discrete vibratory surfaces. 3,814,864. June 4, 1974.

Hearing aid receiver with plural transducers. 4,109,116. August 22, 1978.

Title Index

Resistor and making the same. 2,416,599.
Sound reproducer. 3,478,840.
Transducer hearing aid coupling. 3,118,023.
Vacuum tube with filamentary cathode. 2,462,441.
X-ray measuring instrument. 2,190,200.

VLADIMIR ZWORYKIN (1889-1982)

Electric high-frequency signaling apparatus. 1,484,049.
February 19, 1924.

Wireless transmitting system. 1,634,390. July 5, 1927.

Thermocouple. 1,643,734. September 27, 1927.

Cathode construction for thermionic devices. 1,657,986.
January 31, 1928.

Photoelectric cell. 1,677,316. July 17, 1928.

Making resistance devices. 1,682,547. August 28, 1928.

Television system. 1,689,847. October 30, 1928.

Television system. 1,691,324. November 13, 1928.

Mercury-arc device. 1,696,023. December 18, 1928.

Variable light source. 1,709,647. April 16, 1929.

Interferometer microphone. 1,709,762. April 16, 1929.

Light-responsive relay. 1,709,763. April 16, 1929.

Television system. 1,715,732. June 4, 1929.

Pumping system for metal-tank rectifiers. 1,716,160. June 4, 1929. [With E. B. Shand.]

Photographic sound recording. 1,732,874. October 22, 1929.

Traffic supervisor. 1,743,175. January 14, 1930. [With Roy J. Wensley.]

Oscillator. 1,744,192. January 21, 1930.

Signaling system. 1,753,961. April 8, 1930.

Photoelectric device. 1,763,207. June 10, 1930.

Facsimile transmission system. 1,786,812. December 30, 1930.

Wireless picture transmission. 1,800,000. April 7, 1931.

System for recording electrical fluctuations. 1,802,747. April 28, 1931.

Light sensitive element. 1,807,056. May 26, 1931.

Television apparatus. 1,817,502. August 4, 1931.

Photographic printing apparatus. 1,826,858. October 13, 1931.

Photoelectric tube. 1,832,607. November 17, 1931.

Sound recording and reproducing system. 1,834,197. December 1, 1931.

Photoelectric tube. 1,837,744. December 22, 1931.

Vacuum tube. 1,837,745. December 22, 1931.

Photoelectric tube. 1,837,746. December 22, 1931.

Mercury arc device with grid control. 1,856,087. May 3, 1932. [With D. Ulrey.]

View transmission system. 1,863,363. June 14, 1932.

Frequency-responsive crystal relay. 1,869,829. August 2, 1932. [With Albert M. Skellett.]

Traffic supervisor. Reissue 18,567. August 9, 1932. [With Roy J. Wensley.]

Television apparatus. 1,870,702. August 9, 1932.

Photocell amplifier. 1,872,381. August 16, 1932. [With H. A. Iams.]

Combination of a phototube and an amplifier. 1,883,926. October 25, 1932. [With Harley Iams.]

Light sensitive tube. 1,893,573. January 10, 1933.

Facsimile receiver. 1,909,142. May 16, 1933.

Inspection device. 1,922,188. August 15, 1933.

Oscillation generator. 1,930,499. October 17, 1933.

Photoelectric tube. 1,939,531. December 12, 1933.

Kerr cell. 1,939,532. December 12, 1933.

Method and system for communication by television. 1,955,899. April 24, 1934.

Facsimile-transmission system. Reissue 19,314. September 11, 1934.

Sorting apparatus. 1,979,722. November 6, 1934.

Cathode ray apparatus. 1,988,469. January 22, 1935.

Recording system. 1,996,449. April 2, 1935.

Indicating device. 2,013,594. September 3, 1935.

Television system. 2,017,883. October 22, 1935.

Method of and apparatus for producing images of objects. 2,021,907. November 26, 1935.

Television system. 2,022,450. November 26, 1935.

System for reception by television. 2,025,143. December 24, 1935.

Electrical communication system. 2,028,857. January 28, 1936.

Electric discharge device. 2,078,304. April 27, 1937.

Television system. 2,084,364. June 22, 1937.

Electrical device. 2,085,406. June 29, 1937.

Direction indicator. 2,103,507. December 28, 1937.

Television system. 2,104,066. January 4, 1938.

Television system. 2,107,464. February 8, 1938.

Vacuum tube. 2,109,245. February 22, 1938.

Ultrahigh frequency radio system. 2,125,977. August 9, 1938.

Television system. 2,133,882. October 18, 1938.

Cathode ray tube. 2,139,296. December 6, 1938.

Television system. 2,141,059. December 20, 1938.

Electron multiplier device. 2,144,239. January 17, 1939.

Intelligence transmission system. 2,146,876. February 14, 1939.

Electron multiplier device. 2,147,825. February 21, 1939.

Electric discharge device. 2,150,573. March 14, 1939. [With L. Malter.]

Television system. 2,157,048. May 2, 1939.

Electric discharge device. 2,157,585. May 9, 1939.

Method and apparatus for detecting heat. 2,159,755. May 23, 1939.

Electrical device. 2,159,937. May 23, 1939.

Cathode ray device. 2,168,892. August 8, 1939.

High-frequency oscillator. 2,173,193. September 19, 1939.

Television system. 2,178,093. October 31, 1939. [With G. N. Ogloblinsky.]

Radio course indicator. 2,183,634. December 19, 1939.

Electric discharge device. 2,189,305. February 6, 1940.

Picture transmitter tube. 2,201,215. May 21, 1940.

Electric discharge device. 2,205,055. June 18, 1940. [With L. Malter.]

Television system. 2,206,654. July 2, 1940.

Electron multiplier. 2,231,697. February 11, 1941. [With R. L. Snyder, Jr.]

Electron multiplier. 2,231,698. February 11, 1941. [With J. A. Rajchman.]

Secondary electron emissive electrode. 2,233,276. February 25, 1941. [With H. W. Leverenz and J. E. Ruedy.]

Photoelectric mosaic. 2,246,283. June 17, 1941.

Electron tube. 2,249,552. July 15, 1941.

Television system. 2,280,877. April 28, 1942.

Vacuum plumbing. 2,284,710. June 2, 1942.

View-transmission system. 2,285,551. June 9, 1942.

Electron gun. 2,289,952. July 14, 1942.

Power transmitting mechanism. 2,296,695. September 22, 1942.

Telelectroscope. 2,304,755. December 8, 1942.

View-transmission system. 2,338,562. January 4, 1944.

Dynamic method for correcting the spherical aberration of electron lenses. 2,354,287. July 25, 1944. [With E. G. Ramberg.]

Facsimile-transmission system. 2,361,255. October 24, 1944.

Television system. 2,415,059. January 28, 1947.

Convection current responsive instrument. 2,440,189. April 20, 1948.

Cathode-ray storage tube apparatus and method of operation. 2,451,005. October 12, 1948. [With Paul K. Weimer and I. Wolff.]

Optophone. 2,451,014. October 12, 1948. [With J. Hillier.]

Electronic reading aid for the blind. 2,457,099. December 21, 1948. [With L. E. Flory.]

Color television. 2,566,713. September 4, 1951.

Apparatus for indicia recognition. 2,616,983. November 4, 1952. [With L. E. Flory.]

Electronic simulator. 2,711,289. June 21, 1955.

Color television image reproduction. 2,725,420. November 29, 1955.

Secret television systems. 2,757,226. July 31, 1956.

Color television image reproducing systems. 2,806,899. September 17, 1957.

Automatic control system for vehicles. 2,847,080. August 12, 1958.

Color receiver utilizing velocity modulation in display tube. 2,989,582. June 20, 1961. [With J. A. Rajchman and E. G. Ramberg.]

Color kinescopes and methods of making the same. 3,003,873. October 10, 1961.

Apparatus for meteorological exploration. 3,038,154. June 5, 1962.

Voltage sensing apparatus. 3,052,232. September 4, 1962. [With F. L. Hatke.]

Magnetic recording and reproducing means. 3,072,751. January 8, 1963. [With P. K. Weimer.]

Magnetic record reproducing apparatus. 3,213,206. October 19, 1965. [With P. K. Weimer.]

Photosensitive information retrieval device. 3,215,843. November 2, 1965.

Title Index

Cathode construction for thermionic devices. 1,657,986.

Cathode ray apparatus. 1,988,469.

Cathode ray device. 2,168,892.

Cathode-ray storage tube apparatus and method of operation. 2,451,005.

Cathode ray tube. 2,139,296.

Color receiver utilizing velocity modulation in display tube. 2,989,582.

Color television. 2,566,713.

Color television image reproducing systems. 2,806,899.

Color television image reproduction. 2,725,420.

Color kinescopes and methods of making the same. 3,003,873.

Combination of a phototube and an amplifier. 1,883,926.

Convection current responsive instrument. 2,440,189.

Direction indicator. 2,103,507.

Dynamic method for correcting the spherical aberration of electron lenses. 2,354,287.

Electric discharge device. 2,078,304; 2,150,573; 2,157,585; 2,189,305; 2,205,055.

Electric high-frequency signaling apparatus. 1,484,049.

Electrical communication system. 2,028,857.

Electrical device. 2,085,406; 2,159,937.

Electron gun. 2,289,952.

Electron multiplier. 2,231,697; 2,231,698.

Electron multiplier device. 2,144,239; 2,147,825.

Electron tube. 2,249,552.

Electronic reading aid for the blind. 2,457,099.

Electronic simulator. 2,711,289.

Facsimile receiver. 1,909,142.

Facsimile transmission system. 1,786,812; 2,361,255.

Facsimile-transmission system. Reissue 19,314. September 11, 1934.

Frequency-responsive crystal relay. 1,869,829.

High-frequency oscillator. 2,173,193.

Indicating device. 2,013,594.

Inspection device. 1,922,188.

Intelligence transmission system. 2,146,876.
Interferometer microphone. 1,709,762.
Kerr cell. 1,939,532.
Light-responsive relay. 1,709,763.
Light sensitive element. 1,807,056.
Light sensitive tube. 1,893,573.
Magnetic record reproducing apparatus. 3,213,206.
Magnetic recording and reproducing means. 3,072,751.
Making resistance devices. 1,682,547.
Mercury-arc device. 1,696,023.
Mercury arc device with grid control. 1,856,087.
Method and apparatus for detecting heat. 2,159,755.
Method and system for communication by television.
    1,955,899.
Method of and apparatus for producing images of objects.
    2,021,907.
Optophone. 2,451,014.
Oscillation generator. 1,930,499.
Oscillator. 1,744,192.
Photocell amplifier. 1,872,381.
Photoelectric cell. 1,677,316.
Photoelectric device. 1,763,207.
Photoelectric mosaic. 2,246,283.
Photoelectric tube. 1,832,607; 1,837,744; 1,837,746;
    1,939,531.
Photographic printing apparatus. 1,826,858.
Photographic sound recording. 1,732,874.
Photosensitive information retrieval device. 3,215,843.
Picture transmitter tube. 2,201,215.
Power transmitting mechanism. 2,296,695.
Pumping system for metal-tank rectifiers. 1,716,160.
Radio course indicator. 2,183,634.
Recording system. 1,996,449.
Secondary electron emissive electrode. 2,233,276.
Secret television systems. 2,757,226.
Signaling system. 1,753,961.

Sorting apparatus. 1,979,722.
Sound recording and reproducing system. 1,834,197.
System for reception by television. 2,025,143.
System for recording electrical fluctuations. 1,802,747.
Telelectroscope. 2,304,755.
Television apparatus. 1,817,502; 1,870,702.
Television system. 1,689,847; 1,691,324; 1,715,732;
    2,017,883; 2,022,450; 2,084,364; 2,104,066; 2,107,464;
    2,133,882; 2,141,059; 2,157,048; 2,178,093; 2,206,654;
    2,280,877; 2,415,059.
Thermocouple. 1,643,734.
Traffic supervisor. 1,743,175.
Traffic supervisor. Reissue 18,567. August 9, 1932.
Ultrahigh frequency radio system. 2,125,977.
Vacuum plumbing. 2,284,710.
Vacuum tube. 1,837,745; 2,109,245.
Variable light source. 1,709,647.
View transmission system. 1,863,363; 2,285,551; 2,338,562.
Voltage sensing apparatus. 3,052,232.
Wireless picture transmission. 1,800,000.
Wireless transmitting system. 1,634,390.

How to Get Copies of Patents

Copies of patents may be ordered from the Commissioner of Patents and Trademarks, Washington, DC 20231. Since patents in the U.S. system each have a unique number, copies may be ordered by patent number only. As of November 1991, copies cost $1.50 each.

Patent Depository Libraries

Patents may also be consulted and photocopied at Patent Depository Libraries, listed below. Query libraries before visiting them, since not all of them have complete collections of patent publications.

Alabama	Auburn University Libraries
	Birmingham Public Library
Alaska	Anchorage Municipal Libraries
Arizona	Tempe: Arizona State University
Arkansas	Little Rock: Arkansas State Library
California	Los Angeles Public Library
	Sacramento: California State Library
	San Diego Public Library
	Sunnyvale: Patent Information Clearinghouse
Colorado	Denver Public Library
Connecticut	New Haven: Science Park Library

Delaware	Newark: University of Delaware Library
D.C.	Washington: Howard University Libraries
Florida	Fort Lauderdale: Broward County Library Miami-Dade Public Library Orlando: University of Central Florida Libraries
Georgia	Atlanta: Price Gilbert Memorial Library, Georgia Institute of Technology
Idaho	Moscow: University of Idaho Library
Illinois	Chicago Public Library Springfield: Illinois State Library
Indiana	Indianapolis-Marion County Public Library
Iowa	Des Moines: State Library of Iowa
Kentucky	Louisville Free Public Library
Louisiana	Baton Rouge: Troy H. Middleton Library, Louisiana State University
Maryland	College Park: Engineering and Physical Sciences Library, University of Maryland
Massachusetts	Amherst: Physical Sciences Library, University of Massachusetts Boston Public Library
Michigan	Ann Arbor: Engineering-Transportation Library, University of Michigan Detroit Public Library

Minnesota	Minneapolis Public Library
Missouri	Kansas City: Linda Hall Library St. Louis Public Library
Montana	Butte: Montana College of Mineral Science and Technology Library
Nebraska	Lincoln: Engineering Library, University of Nebraska-Lincoln
Nevada	Reno: University of Nevada-Reno Library
New Hampshire	Durham: University of New Hampshire Library
New Jersey	Newark Public Library Piscataway: Library of Science and Medicine at Rutgers University
New Mexico	Albuquerque: University of New Mexico Library
New York	Albany: New York State Library Buffalo and Erie County Public Library New York Public Library
North Carolina	Raleigh: D. H. Hill Library, North Carolina State University
Ohio	Cincinnati & Hamilton County Public Library Cleveland Public Library Columbus: Ohio State University Libraries Toledo/Lucas County Public Library

Oklahoma	Stillwater: Oklahoma State University Library
Oregon	Salem: Oregon State Library
Pennsylvania	Philadelphia Free Library Pittsburgh: Carnegie Library University Park: Pattee Library, Pennsylvania State University
Rhode Island	Providence Public Library
South Carolina	Charleston: Medical University of South Carolina Library
Tennessee	Memphis & Shelby County Public Library Nashville: Vanderbilt University Library
Texas	Austin: McKinney Engineering Library, University of Texas at Austin College Station: Sterling C. Evans Library, Texas A & M University Dallas Public Library Houston: Fondren Library, Rice University
Utah	Salt Lake City: Marriott Library, University of Utah
Virginia	Richmond: Virginia Commonwealth University Library
Washington	Seattle: Engineering Library, University of Washington
West Virginia	Morgantown: Wise Library, West Virginia University

| Wisconsin | Madison: Library, University of Wisconsin-Madison |
| | Milwaukee Public Library |

PERSONAL NAME INDEX